Second Edition

Understanding Cultural Diversity in Today's Complex World

Dr. Leo Parvis

To all who make our world diverse,
To the parents of our younger generations,
To my sweetheart Julie,
To all educators of diversity,
To advocates of human rights and diversity,
To all diverse people who make America beautiful,
To messengers of peace, humanity, and brotherhood,
To all positive people,
To you, and us,
To generations to come,
I dedicate this book.

Acknowledgements

There is no significant accomplishment without teamwork. Therefore, all of those who participated to help get the job done must be acknowledged for their hard work, support, and perseverance. My first appreciation goes to my wife Julie for her hard work in editing the manuscript, her production work, her support, and encouragement, especially during the darkest days of writing. A huge thank you to our dear friend Cristine Grimm for her technical and emotional support, you are the best! A special thank you to Juanita Nanez, Vice President of Diversity, Carlson Restaurants Worldwide, for taking the time to read the book and providing me with useful feedback and changes. I really appreciate your time and consideration. Julie's aunt Dr. Jan Meyer and parents David & Judy Anderson were the first supporters of this text by giving good advice, guidance, and a place to escape and write! My former department director Dr. Steve Ivancic should also be acknowledged for his continuous support and encouragement. I would also like to thank Dr. Ben Wright, President of Dunwoody College, for reading the text and providing the foreword. I must confess that the list of supporters is very large. To make it short, I would like to thank all my family, friends, and human rights colleagues who waited for two years to see this text published. God be with all of you.

Dr. Leo Parvis
August 2005
Minneapolis, MN

Contents

Part Two: Our Social Interactions

Chapter 4: Diversity and Reactive Syndromes

Chapter 5: The Challenges and Benefits of Diversity

The Challenges:

The Benefits:

Chapter 6: A Quest for Recognition

Chapter 7: Interaction in the Realm of Diversity

Chapter 8: Diversity and Personal Conduct

Part Three: Power Distance and Human Sensitivity

Chapter 9: Diversity and Human Rights

Foreword

*D*iversity is one of those words loaded with emotional connotations that can evoke charges of "political correctness" on the one hand and equally strong defenses of "social justice" and "human equality" on the other. Frankly, I have never really been able to understand the passionate feelings generated by diversity education -- first, because it is indisputable that the United States is one of the most culturally diverse nations in the world; and, second, since our nation is so diverse, **not** to teach diversity in our schools and colleges would seem to be a colossal act of denial.

Even before the founding of the United States of America, this land had been incredibly diverse, with a multiplicity of Native American nations and cultures. The arrival of European conquerors and settlers simply added to the cultural diversity of the continent. Contributing even more ethnic complexity to our American heritage was the introduction of African slaves as an integral part of the colonization process. Then, during the 19th century, as the young United States of America absorbed ever increasing numbers of immigrants from different countries of Europe, some Americans began to speak of an American "melting pot." Although the "melting pot" was always more myth than reality, it recognized the obvious ethnic and religious diversity of the expanding new nation.

As so-called "newer immigrants" began to fill American cities in the early years of the 20th century, a movement paralleled by the beginning of a mass migration of African Americans from the rural South into large Northern cities, more established groups began to resist both immigration and social equality for non-white peoples. Prejudice and discrimination were not uncommon at a time when the population was changing visibly. Remarkably, in largely Caucasian Minneapolis, Minnesota, a prominent business leader founded a unique trade school in 1914 founded on the principle of social and religious equality, at the very time when a system of racial segregation was being re-introduced in our nation's capital. William Hood Dunwoody, founder of Dunwoody College of Technology, established a school whose purpose would be to provide education for the youth of Minnesota *"without distinction on account of race, color or religious prejudice."* Although the new college did not immediately enroll people of color or women, it did enroll immigrants and low-income students at a time when other Minnesota colleges did not provide educational opportunity for persons of such diverse backgrounds.

The 20th century witnessed the continuing evolution of diversity as a force in American society and politics. Although the American electorate rejected an Irish-American Catholic candidate for President in 1928, the election of Franklin D. Roosevelt in 1932 and the creation of FDR's "New Deal coalition" of new immigrants, labor unions, African Americans, and the underemployed dominated American politics into the 1960's.

Since the 1960's, other immigrant groups – Mexicans, Southeast Asians, Somalis, Ethiopians, Russian Jews, and others – have brought an even wider array of languages, religions, and cultures into the American mix. In addition, the so-called "Women's Liberation" movement of the 1970's (which had been preceded by a women's rights movement of the 19th century and the suffragette movement of the early 20th century) introduced gender into the social and political landscape. And, more recently, the issue of sexual orientation has become yet another element of our complex multicultural society.

As educators, we must recognize all of the facets of the human beings who make up our student populations. Our students are male or female. They subscribe to different religions or no religion. They have unique national origins. They are members of one race or several races. They have particular sexual orientations. They have different political views. Some are rich, some are poor. Some are young, some are older. Some have physical limitations. All learn in different ways -- some by doing, others by listening, watching, or reading. We can deny that these differences exist, we can actively suppress differences, or we can accept differences as a reality and learn from others who are different from ourselves.

By analyzing diversity and the various facets of a multicultural society, Dr. Parvis's book helps us celebrate diversity. Like our founder, William Hood Dunwoody, we at Dunwoody College of Technology believe that diversity is a value worthy of understanding and active support. Indeed, one of the college's strategic goals is *"to create and sustain a college environment that encourages and nurtures diversity."* We believe that all of our lives are enriched when we appreciate the differences of others.

Dr. C. Ben Wright, President
Dunwoody College of Technology
Minneapolis, MN

Introduction

People are still not embracing the concept of diversity. It is an immediate concern of social and behavioral scientists to educate people as much as possible in order to minimize ignorance and false assumptions. Some habits contribute to baseless judgments and biased arguments such as negativity and obliviousness. America is a unique country in the world. A majority of Americans believe: "We are the world." People from every part of the world have chosen the United States to be their home. We all live and work together regardless of our national origin, religion, ethnicity, political ideology, and sexual orientation. We all live and work together for our prosperity and for keeping America number one in all aspects of life.

The main purpose of writing this text originated from the attitude of "Teach Me What I Need to Know in My Limited Time" that is prevalent in most colleges in the United States. In doing so, I intend to address the most applicable cultural diversity topics and issues that are useful not only for college students but for everyone in this country.

Our political leaders, human rights activists, and many academic authorities have put an emphasis on promoting cultural diversity education at the college level. Therefore, it is time to set forth a universal aspect to cultural diversity and recommend that all colleges and universities teach these aspects as an integral part of their curricula. This text will well serve the purpose for many who decide to learn and teach the fundamentals of cultural diversity. The primary target for this textbook is college students. It is also beneficial for high school juniors and seniors whose educators have realized the importance of teaching about cultural diversity. Non-academic organizations and diverse workforces whose goals are permeated with valuing diversity initiatives should find this text useful.

It should also be noted that this book does not intend to generate a feeling that one particular group is being attacked or singled out for issues or agitations of the diversity we encounter in this society. In order to be successful in social life and business, we need to bear in mind that cultural diversity should always be looked at positively as a means of growth and a way to sustain harmony—

harmony for a nation that is united in faith and trust to preserve justice and equality for all.

In this book, I have tried to include most diversity related subjects which everybody needs to know in a multicultural society like ours. Starting with culture, diversity, and the transition from melting pot to a multicultural setting, the first part presents the most crucial part of the text, that is, the images and realities. In the second part, I have presented the most controversial issues of diversity, namely reactive syndromes, challenges and benefits, black America's quest for recognition, and interaction in the realm of diversity. In this part, readers need to realize that personal conduct is a vital element of living in a diverse society. Civility and ethics are the most needed human characteristics in dealing with different cultural backgrounds. In part three, I found it necessary to value the significance of human rights here at home and around the world. This last section of the book demonstrates a reality that is the humiliation of humanity by almost two-thirds of the world's countries. Violation of human rights in many countries, including the United States, is not known by most Americans and other citizens of the world. In the last chapter, the concept of globalization and the future of diversity in America and around the world give a directive path towards the future and the years ahead for our new generation. The message is to embrace diversity and be proud of the human race for which Mankind is One.

Poems are always good sources of knowledge, understanding, and constructive messages. I have included selected poems and song lyrics related to diversity throughout the text. A selected number of "Quotable Quotes" are also included throughout the text to ensure that readers have more access to words of wisdom from different perspectives. Last but not least, it is always helpful to have a quick reference and know the meaning of words used in the text. Thus, a glossary was put together which is an integral part of an academic text. I am always grateful for readers' feedback and suggestions for improvement and better quality. This has been a challenging experience and we all learn from our past experiences.

Leo Parvis, Ph.D.
Minneapolis, MN
July, 2005

PART ONE

Images and Realities

Chapter 1: Culture

"Preservation of one's own culture does not require
contempt or disrespect for other cultures."

-Cesar Chavez
Hispanic civil rights and labor leader

Objectives

- Define culture
- Compare and contrast different meanings of culture
- Explore cultural differences
- Identify culture shocks
- Discuss culture in American society
- Examine the influence of sub-cultures

What is Culture?

Culture is a complex term due to the fact that it does not
present a fixed meaning. People's perception of culture varies from
place to place—that is called the world view which is a product of
culture. Culture is the way of life of a group of people. It forms a
person's life through influences that are available to everybody
through the circle of humanity that is surrounding the individual at the
center. Traditions, values, and criteria within the realm of family,
friends, and other elements of influence shape one's culture.

Briefly, anthropologists define culture in a way that explains
learned behavior. E. B. Taylor, the first professional anthropologist,
defines culture as a variety of human experience: "Culture…is that
complex whole which includes knowledge, belief, arts, morals, law,
custom, and any other capabilities and habits acquired by man as a
member of society (Scupin, 2003)." In other words, as Laroche (2003,
p. 68) puts it, "culture includes an implicit list of standard operating
procedures." Those who have talked about culture interpret it as a
realm that is comprised of traditional ideas, related values, and
demonstrated behaviors. William Sonnenschein (1997) asserts that
culture is learned, shared, and transmitted from one generation to the
next and that it organizes life and helps interpret existence.

Furthermore, culture is a set of custom rules a group of people have learned to respond to life's events, such as deaths, births or weddings.

Culture is comprised of those characteristics of human life that are different from place to place. The most apparent of all these characteristics are language, traditions, food, clothes, arts, dance, music, and sports. Other characteristics of culture are invisible such as concept of time, religion, political ideology, friendship, beauty, sin, and education to name a few.

Shepard (1996) asserts that if you understand culture you have the opportunity to elevate your awareness of your own culture as well as the culture of other people.

Lindsey and Beach (2002, p. 59), offer a useful definition of culture: "Human behavior is immensely varied, and the variations are fundamentally determined by culture. Culture is a human society's total way of life; it is learned and shared and includes the society's values, customs, material objects, and symbols." Accordingly, every person's culture includes his or her social heritage that tells them which behaviors are appropriate and which are not.

Those norms and styles of life that we learn as we grow are indicative of our learned characteristics of customary life. Our parents, as immediate teachers and role models, have a great deal of impact on our personalities and the culture we build along the line of growth. They are similar to masons or bricklayers of a structure who put their hearts and minds into the work or the duty they are committed to accomplish. If the structure is laid with flaws, chances are that the shape would be slanted as it is erected. Some grandparents contribute to the upbringing of their grandchildren, yet it varies from culture to culture. The words of wisdom they enunciate provide a valuable groundwork for our future endeavors. In fact, our close association with our family circles, and our locality teach us many historical facts about our past generations. "All known prehistoric and historic societies are thought to have common features, called **cultural universals**, that aided in their survival" (Lindsey & Beach, 2002, p. 72). Accordingly, more than 50 years ago, George Murdoch, an anthropologist who is known for his list of more than seventy cultural universals, introduced features such as family patterns, food taboos, religious rituals, ethics, folklore, and decorative arts, to name a few. An example of a cultural universal is *the taboo of incest*—referring to restrictions of sexual relations and marriage between blood-related individuals (Murdoch, 1945). As most anthropologists and sociologists have observed, culture is always changing.

Due to human nature and life fluctuations, every culture is, at a snail's pace, on the move. Some examples of cultural change are: creativity and innovation within a cultural group, alteration, modification, and transformation in the physical environment, revolutionizing the fabric of society, and last but not least, interaction with other cultures. In some religious societies (Christian, Islamic, etc.), culture is saturated in the realm of religion. In most Islamic countries, religion plays an important role in shaping the society. In some, for example The Islamic Republic of Iran, where religion is fundamental to society, resistance is prevalent and nationalists who respect their culture, traditions, and heritage have a mental struggle to dichotomize the religion and culture and persist to draw a line between the two.

The character of a culture is defined by **values** that help us know what to do, but not necessarily how to do it. **Norms**, on the other hand, are rules of conduct that guide our behavior in specific situations. **Etiquette** is defined as the practices and forms prescribed by social convention or by authority (American Heritage, 1996). Within every system of culture, social manners are taught by elders as children grow up. Some parents, inadvertently, do not teach these manners to their youngsters. Teachers may fill the gaps as children receive compulsory education. Otherwise, the lack of etiquette and civility may cause some embarrassment and discomfort in later years. More on personal conduct and etiquette will be discussed in chapter 8.
More Definitions of Culture:

- The totality of socially transmitted behavior patterns, arts, beliefs, institutions, and all other products of human work and thought (American Heritage College Dictionary, 1993).
- Culture or ethnic groups represent associate belief and behavior systems that are passed down from one generation to the next through learning (Hogan-Garcia, 2003).
- The characteristic customs, social patterns, beliefs, and values of people in a particular country or region, or in a particular racial or religious group (Cascio, 2003).
- A system of values, beliefs, notions about acceptable and unacceptable behavior, and other socially

constructed ideas characteristic of a society or subgroup within a society (Garcia, 2002).

- Culture is learned behavior, constrained by inherited capacities that give general directions for specific and flexible behavior. Culture refers to values, ideas, expectations, things we make, clothing we wear, behavior we express. Culture shapes how we see things, what we make of what we see, and how we feel about it. We adapt to different environments and situations through culture. We survive with culture, perish without it (Middleton, 2003).

- Culture consists of material objects as well as the patterns for thinking, feeling, and behaving that are passed from generation to generation among members of a society (Shepard, 2003).

- Culture is often viewed as the behaviors, beliefs, values and attitudes of various groups. Broadly defined, culture can be defined as the way things are done within any group (Heuberger, 2001).

- Culture derives from the Latin root colare, and is associated with activities of preservation, of tending to and caring for (Benhabib, 2002).

Cultural Differences

Cultural differences have always been critical and controversial. The main reason for this argument lies within the lack of knowledge and understanding of cultures and the misconception of race and ethnicity. Those who seek cultural diversity education should be able to distinguish the distinction between race and ethnicity as they explore cultural differences.

People are confused when it comes to race and ethnicity. Most sociologists make a clear distinction between race and ethnicity. Appropriately, race is a matter of social construct, and not an established biological concept (Heuberger, 2001). In other words, **race** is a social construct that unnaturally divides people into distinct groups based on characteristics such as physical appearance (particularly color), ancestral heritage, and socioeconomic needs (Adams, et al., 1997). Some examples of race according to the U.S. Census classification of race includes, but not limited to, "White [Caucasian],

Black, Indian, Eskimo, Aleut, Asian or Pacific Islander, Chinese, Filipino, Hawaiian, Korean, Vietnamese, Japanese, Asian Indian, Samoan, Guamanian, other." **Ethnicity** is truly a matter of culture. It is related to many aspects of culture such as language, behavioral patterns, religion, traditions, heritage, and geographic origins. Sometimes, ethnicity and religion are mixed and make an exception such as in the case of Judaism—Jewish is a faith and an ethnicity. Social scientists have clearly distinguished human groups based on culture rather than race. "For example, when they refer to tribal groupings within the border racial category of Native Americans as separate ethnic groups, they are emphasizing cultural differences in defining group identity as opposed to biological or physical ones" (Diller, 1999, p. 49). A good example is Native American tribes which provided different rules and teachings for up-bringing their offspring.

It is best for all of us not to confuse ourselves with the term race and focus on cultural differences that are the focal point of diversity.

Middleton (2003) explains that "There's a great tendency to see groups of people in terms of their differences from us. They look different, act different, speak a different language. When they say and do things that we do not like, we attribute it to who they are—to the idea that they are different in an essential way." (p. 64)

Variation in the ways of life, ideology, traditions, clothing, arts, music, concept of time, and many other factors provide a basis for differences among cultures. Because of these differences, and the ethnocentric assumption that others see the world in the same way as we do, people are confronted with cross-cultural misunderstanding. Cultures put forth such a powerful influence that many people demonstrate **ethnocentrism**, the tendency or belief in the superiority of one's own ethnic group. In other words, ethnocentrism is judging other groups by the values of one's own group. In chapter three, we shall read more on ethnocentrism.

Cultural differences can be found in differing living conditions, relationships, emotions, working styles, teaching, raising children, and ruling a society, to name a few. There are many cultural differences. Simply, some ways of life or habits that are practiced in eastern cultures may seem bizarre in western cultures, and vice-versa.

For instance, shows of emotion are not welcomed in many cultures. Conversely, in the American culture, it is not only considered healthy, it may be beneficial to a circle of friends, a team, or to the organization we work for (Sonnenschein, 1997).

In Asia there are many cultures that are quite different in norms and values within Asian societies and that of the western world as well. Two prominent Asian cultures that emigrated to the United States in the 1840s are the Chinese and Japanese whose challenges and successes have become historical highlights of American cultural diversity. Ronald Takaki (1993) in *A Different Mirror: A History of Multicultural America*, describes the voices of non-Anglo peoples (Native Americans, African Americans, Irish Americans, Jewish Americans, Asian Americans, Latinos, and others) who contributed to shaping America with all their differences. These differences brought creativity, innovations, and a uniqueness that made America what it is today.

One of the characteristics of culture is **food** which acts as a conduit that connects people from all ethnicities and backgrounds. Food, anywhere in the world, functions as the first level of acceptance. Ethnic restaurants, everywhere, are the clearinghouse of traditions. People experience the food without even knowing a person of the culture. Diana Abu-Jaber (2003), in her recent romantic novel about an Arab-American girl originally from Iraq, residing in the heart of an Iranian neighborhood (Iran-geles), in Los Angeles, speaks about food as a cultural phenomenon. In *Crescent: A Romance in Iran-geles*, Abu-Jaber exemplifies food as one of the most immediate and most convincing ways of explaining cultural experience to another person.

Cultural differences are depicted in numerous forms of communication. We learn from mass media on a daily basis. No boundary is known when it comes to culture. In other words, cultural differences are not associated with different nations and countries only. They occur within a race, an ethnicity, or a region. Arabs of the Middle Eastern countries may have a factor of cohesiveness and unification, at least in theory, such as Islamic religion, and Arabic that is the language of their holy book *Koran*, yet they portray many differences vis-à-vis culture. From North Africa, to South Africa, and from eastern shores to western coasts of Africa, we may find many ethnicities with different religious and ritual practices mixed with various lifestyles.

It is an amazing world of differences pertaining to cultures. The more you know about cultures, the better you can interact with people from different backgrounds. Obviously, if differences are not reconciled, relationships will be disputed and conflicts are inevitable. Extreme cultural difference may lead to "culture wars." Amitai Etzioni in his remarkable work *the New Golden Rule* (Etzioni, 1996) asserts: "Culture wars lead to divisiveness, a lack of resolution on overdue issues ("gridlock"), intergroup hatred, and tribalism." (p. 101)

Along differences, there are commonalities among cultures in the world too. For instance, in the Islamic world, religion is a factor of commonality. The Arab world represents a variety of cultures, yet two obvious similarities are language and religion. They speak Arabic, and practice Islam. It should be mentioned that in the Islamic religion, followers of Shia and Suni represent two different paths in Islam. It is also important to say that religion in the Islamic world plays an important role in decision making and setting standards. Some Islamic governments take advantage of their people by influencing the power of religion in devising laws and regulations.

In summary, it is important to mention about cultural differences when we talk about diversity. Cultural differences appear in social interactions, working together, or sharing a common cause. Workplaces in the United States have become increasingly multicultural in recent years. Tension and misunderstanding arise in workplaces where people from different backgrounds and national origins have to spend time together for many hours under one roof. Today's workforces in North America consist of a variety of minorities from many parts of the world, mostly Hispanics, Asians, Europeans, Eastern Europeans, people from the Far East, and people from the Middle East, not to mention Native Americans, and African Americans. These culturally different workers represent diverse attitudes and various socio-economic standards which from time to time may lead to problems among workers and employers. It has become a common phrase these days to be "culturally competent."

Culture Shock

Culture shock happens when we observe actions or behaviors that are totally different from our own. Ostensibly, any different norm, event, or style of life that is foreign to an individual would be a culture shock when another culture is visited or experienced. Middleton (2003), in the book *The Challenge of Human Diversity*, indicates that people complain about the ways of life in other cultures when they visit a country. For example, American travelers usually complain about air, water, food, means of transportation, bathrooms, odor, and the list can go on forever. Americans are so careful of their health, so as not to get sick when visiting another part of the world which does not have immediate medical care as in America (Middleton, 2003).

What is American Culture?

When speaking of American culture, we intend to refer to the main stream culture in the United States. Some argue that there is no specific culture as "American Culture." Diller (1999) makes it more clear when he talks about culture and cultural difference:

> "My white students often complain that they have no culture: they know nothing and feel nothing about where they came from. What they mean, I believe, is that they lack the kind of connection to a cultural heritage and community that they see among People of Color and White ethnics (p.47)."

There are numerous characteristics of culture that are associated with Americans. Wearing jeans is a product of American culture. Jazz music, country western music, rock and blue grass music are part of American culture. Drinking coke, hot cider and roasting marshmallows on a bon-fire is American. Eating McDonald's hamburgers, playing football and baseball, are considered part of American culture. Fourth of July celebrations, a good cultural education around the country, are a fair example of American culture.

America is not only the United States. From Canada to South America is geographically considered "America." This continent consists of many distinctive cultures. For many years it was known as the "American Continent." Modern geographers divide it into two parts—North American and South American continents. History is the theater of cultural performances. The United States, which formally came in to existence and became an independent country in 1776, already was home to many groups of people who came to this land of opportunity in search of prosperity, happiness, and freedom (Takaki, 1993).

Before Christopher Columbus mistakenly landed on American shores, Native Americans were the sole inhabitants of this great land. Columbus' mistake was corrected by Amerigo Vespucci (1454-1512) an Italian explorer of the South American coast who argued that this newly explored land was not India as was previously claimed by Columbus. Therefore, "America" was named in his honor. Genuine Americans are the Native Americans who eventually surrendered land to the pioneers.

The United States is a nation of people with numerous ethnic backgrounds. We all are Americans, regardless of where we came from. Today, most people around the world associate American culture with the many traditions that have traveled to all parts of the world. McDonald's as a result of globalization, Hollywood motion pictures due to remarkable cinematography, and many other innovations and creativities have presented byproducts of American culture.

Those who grew up in main stream America, call themselves Americans and are proud of the culture they built up for more than two centuries. Although the bedrock of the foundation was shaped by Europeans representing different cultures, when they put together the blocks of this great nation, they created a unique culture that resembled a melting pot. Some were not allowed to join, others did not want to join and therefore glorified the pride of retaining their own ethnicities. This resulted in the phenomenon of multiculturalism which will be discussed later.

Sub-Culture

In most sociology texts we find some information about "sub-cultures." Cultural diversity owes much to the assumption that sub-cultures provide a substantial ground to the discussion of diversity in any given society. Particularly in the United States, sub-cultures are prominent and more accessible for research and special studies. A **sub-culture** is a group of people within a culture who practices a unique way of life, based on historical facts or generated through ideologies. In other words, sub-cultures are characteristically based on race, ethnicity, age, gender, profession, ideology, or religion.

Academic institutions in the United States attract many immigrant students and staff from all over the world. In fact they are one of the largest employers of diverse ethnicities (Laroache, 2003). "American college campuses represent an amazing degree of sub-cultural diversity. Colleges are struggling with the issue of celebrating diversity but also valuing unity among their students, whether they are American students or international students" (Lindsey & Beach, 2002).

Native Americans, the Amish, religious groups, distinctive groups such as gays and lesbians, or disabled populations are considered sub-cultures. People with exotic customs, magical beliefs and practices are also among the sub-cultural diverse population.

Summary

Culture is the broad set of values, traditions, historical experiences, kinship structure, and so forth which is a cohesive factor for peoples of a tribe, nation, or a region. Culture is the way of life— the standard operating procedures which form our daily lives. We grow with culture and may change it as we adapt to a new environment for survival, freedom, and perhaps prosperity. Due to significant cultural differences, we encounter unusual habits and practices that are foreign or strange to us. The observation of these unusual behaviors is known as "culture shock," especially when we visit a foreign country with a different life style. America is a unique collection of cultures, yet it presents its own cultural values that all sub-cultures respect and acquire for their working lives. Within the broader culture in America lie many sub-cultures whose race, ethnicity, gender, beliefs, ideas, and occupation indicate the quality of being different and a sense of integrity that is the product of our democracy.

Test Your Knowledge

Part One: Fill in the blanks:
1. Many aspects of diversity create cultural differences. Name four of them.

a………………….....b……………………..c…………………………..
d…………………

2. Give four examples of different aspects of culture that we are programmed by.

a…………………….....b……………………..c…………………………...
d…………………

3. What do we first notice when we first meet someone?

a…………………….....b……………………..c…………………………...
d…………………

Part Two: Select the best choice

Instructions: Place the number next to each statement that is agreeable with your understanding and beliefs.
1. extremely agree   2. somewhat agree   3. somewhat disagree   4. disagree   5. not sure

1. _____ Civility and ethics are linked to cultural norms.
2. _____ In order to understand cultural differences we need to interact with people from different backgrounds.
3. _____ The analogy of parents and masons or brick-layers represents the importance of upbringing of children.
4. _____ Culture is learned and unlearned.
5. _____ Culture does not necessarily make a person successful or unsuccessful.
6. _____ People should be respected for who they are not what culture they represent.
7. _____ Traditions, values, and criteria within the realm of family, friends, and other elements of influence shape one's own culture.
8. _____ No culture is better than the other culture.

9. _____ Culture wars create divisiveness, chaos, and anarchy.

10. _____ The Israeli-Palestinian conflict seems to be more of a culture war than a shooting war.

Part Three: Discussion Questions

1. To learn about your race and ethnicity, what criteria would be instrumental to educate yourself?
2. What factors would you choose to compare and contrast your cultural differences with another person from a different background?
3. How would you prepare yourself if you find out that there will be soon a new neighbor from another country moving into your community?
4. What culture shock have you experienced in your life so far, either by visiting another country or encountering others at your work or school?
5. What is your perception about culture wars? Do you think conflicts are caused by cultural differences or they are the products of political justifications?

"No culture can live, if it attempts to be exclusive."

-Mahatma Gandhi
Hindu nationalist leader (1869-1948)

"Culture is the habit of being pleased with the best and knowing why."

-Henry van Dyke
American Poet

"Culture is but the fine flowering of real education, and it is the training of the feeling, the tastes, and the manners that makes it so."

-Minnie Kellogg,
Native American (Oneida) activist and writer

Chapter 2: Diversity

"The more we let each voice sing out with its own true tone,
the richer will be the diversity of the chant in unison."

-Angelus Silesius (1624-1677)
A Polish-German Poet and Priest

"Diversity: the art of thinking independently together."

-Malcolm Forbes (1919-1990),
A famous American publisher

Objectives

- Define the meaning of diversity
- Identify different types of diversity
- Explore important concepts of diversity
- Discuss the key elements in diversity
- Distinguish the importance of diversity education
- Explore the role of media in diversity

What is Diversity?

In chapter one, we defined culture, explored a variety of definitions of culture, and learned how to define it in our own words. In this chapter, we learn about diversity, different types of diversity, and explore the realm of diversity in general that has been the main topic of discussion in recent years. **Diversity** is defined as the quality of being different. This word is derived from "diverse" meaning differing from one another, or simply composed of distinct elements or qualities. Now, we are dealing with the concept that is the focal point of this book: What is this *diversity* that many people are talking about these days? What and why should we know about diversity? These questions can be answered in many ways. The simplest and foremost answer is to learn how to live and work together without creating any conflict. Many problems are generated from a lack of understanding and awareness. We ought to know more about different cultures in this country. Especially after the tragedy of

September 11, 2001, the loss of more than 3000 lives in the attack on the World Trade Center Twin Towers, the Pentagon, and the plane crash in Pennsylvania, the general public realized that a lack of knowledge about other cultures and ethnicities can become very detrimental to the fabric of our society. The media imposed a great deal of attention on terrorism, the Middle East, and the lives and works of Muslims in the United States, yet we found that we need more academic experts on global studies, especially the Middle East. Furthermore, if Americans, including government authorities, knew more about other cultures and relaxed their individualistic mindset, they could have been prepared and mobilized for the early prevention of such tragedies. It is a prevailing indication that the American public needs more global education and understanding of cultures.

The recent tragedies, conflicts, and engagements of the U.S. troops in Afghanistan and Iraq prompted authorities, educators, and human rights activists to focus more on cultural diversity around the country. Schools, colleges, and universities started teaching courses on diversity, and more workplaces began seminars and mandatory training sessions for their employees.

Diversity is an inevitable phenomenon in North America. The United States of America has been dealing with diversity since the pioneer era. The history of our modern time is the best evidence of diversity that every American should know about. More than 200 years of history reveal how much work has been done to make it possible for people of all backgrounds to live and work together. Needless to say that challenges still exist in all states and in every level of human life.

According to Luhabe (2001), "Diversity is a new culture of human behavior that honors people where they are, with what they know, how they acquired this knowledge, and how they apply it. This could be different for each person." (p. 75) The fact is that diversity is here with us and shall remain for ever. We need to learn how to acknowledge our similarities and at the same time embrace our differences.

Below, Thomas and Aldelfer (1988) express their thoughts about cultural diversity:

> Any observer of contemporary life in organizations must conclude that cultural diversity is an unavoidable part of it. Even communities and societies once thought to be synonymous with homogeneity, such as the Rocky Mountain regions of the western United States, Japan, and Scandinavia, are finding that technology and economic progress necessitate the opening of their physical and psychological boundaries to those who are culturally and ethnically different.

Different Types of Diversity

There are many kinds of diversity to be identified around the globe. In the western world, especially in North America, we encounter many more types of diversity compared to other parts of the world.

We are all different, in one way or the other. Understandably, diversity includes many different attributes including culture, ethnicity, class, gender, religion, age, ability, language, weight, style, idea, income, orientation, geographic location and many more aspects which make people unique.

When the topic of diversity is the theme of discussion many unfamiliar words or concepts may be used. Words and phrases such as inclusion, equity, equal opportunity employer (EOE), affirmative action, harassment, civil rights, women in the workplace, glass ceiling, gays and lesbians, "don't ask, don't tell," minorities, religious practices, anti- defamation, pluralism, harmony, tolerance, and unity, to name a few, are all related to diversity (Arrien, 2001), yet each has its own unique definition and should not be replaced for diversity. Each of these terms will be discussed in later chapters.

In a society as blended as the United States, where a variety of people live in 50 states united as one nation, believing in democracy and justice, diversity demonstrates a spectra of numerous levels of income, living conditions, quality of education, different legislations, different geographic locations, and social norms. Since the 1980s, more than ever, the subject of diversity has been gaining momentum in our society due to the fact that major organizations are realizing that in order to be successful in sales and services we need to educate everybody about diversity in the workplace. In today's workplace one needs to associate with people from many different cultures. Individuals with different religious backgrounds, social styles, and different communication patterns can be found everywhere in our society. The first and foremost thing to do is to accept diversity and seek the ways that make us more comfortable with one another. The main types of diversity which identify people and their associations are explained below:

Race

The race issue in the United States history begins with European pioneers, particularly the English who confiscated the land from the native people. The indigenous people referred to the European intruder as "White Man" as opposed to Native Americans who had darker skins. Later, in early 1600, Africans were brought to this country by Europeans against their will. Subsequently, color of skin was the main indicator of people who also represented different geographic regions of the world. Generally, **race** signifies certain, common and distinguishing physical characteristics comprising a comprehensive class which appears to be derived from a distinct historic source (NOW, 2004).

The topic of race has become a well-known subject all over the United States. Dialogues on race have gained momentum in many areas, including civic and academic. Police brutality is repeatedly questioned about whether or not it relates to racism. Many police chiefs around the country have opened dialogues with their communities to exonerate themselves from the accusation of racism. Needless to say, the Rodney King tragedy of 1991 in Los Angeles, California, brought racism to the forefront again in America.

Ethnicity

Ethnicity denotes a classification or affiliation with a group of people having common customs, characteristics, language, etc. Sometimes people are confused about race and ethnicity. Scupin (2003) states that "One important aspect of culture is the recognition of one's group as distinct from another based on different values, beliefs, norms, and other characteristics. When referring to these differences, anthropologists use the term *ethnic group* and *ethnicity*." (p. 56). One good example of an ethnic group are the Amish people in the United States who have maintained their way of life for centuries to date regardless of high tech modernization not far away from their ambient. It is proper to say that ethnicity is the collective differences we learned from our ancestors via cultural heritage.

Sex

Sex is a biological characteristic and not a social construction. Issues about sex (including sexism and chauvinism) are a worldwide concern which varies from place to place. As a part of diversity challenges, sexism is troublesome in many work places. Women and minorities have been discriminated in their workplaces for promotions and salary raises. The term **glass ceiling** refers to a discrimination that is imposed upon women and minorities. Simply, these individuals are deprived of their rights of getting promoted to a higher level and the subsequent salary designated for a particular position. Women, despite enormous gain in recent years, still account for only 10% of senior management in *Fortune* 500 companies (Meyerson & Fletcher, 2001).

Gender

In recent years the word *gender* has become well established in its use to refer to sex-based categories, as in *the politics of gender*. Many anthropologists have supported this usage. They prefer to use sex for reference to biological categories, and gender while referring to social or cultural categories. The National Organization for Women defines gender in the following manner: *Gender* was not chosen because gender connotes a socially imposed sex-role. One cannot discuss "gender" issues without reference to stereotypes according to biological sex identification (NOW, 2004). The significant point in cultural diversity about gender is the status of males and females in social and political settings. Some female individuals may be deprived and discriminated against due to the fact that traditionally some positions are held by males. Even a male homosexual can be denied a job due to his gender status. In ancient times females have held high social and political positions. Artemis, a female naval commander in chief for the Persian Empire fleet is an example of high office that was not held by a male. This fact has also been proven by anthropologist

Lewis Morgan about what was practiced at some time in the past and reversed through time. Another term that is controversial in our society and should be learned in cultural diversity is Sexual Orientation. Coming out of the closet has been, in some cases, very difficult for some individuals, primarily because of the trepidation and anxiety of not being accepted within family, relatives, and their circle of friends. Sexual orientation has been the subject of discussion for quite sometime in American workplaces, especially the military. In the 1990s, President Clinton supported the policy of "Don't Ask, Don't Tell" to alleviate the hardship existing in the military and other workplaces regarding sexual orientation. Sexual orientation specifically includes lesbian and gay, bisexual and heterosexual people (NOW, 2004).

Geographic Diversity

The world is full of diversity. When you leave your homeland to visit another country you notice the differences quite easily such as landscapes, landmarks, monuments, building structures, locations, and neighborhoods, to name a few. The climate has a great impact on the way people live, think, and behave. This phenomenon has, sometimes, created perceptions mixed with stereotypes. For many years Europeans referred to people from the Middle East as those who ride camels. Similarly, the term "Third World" coined by Europeans referred to those countries with no industrialization. Today, this term is not used very much and has been replaced by "Developing Countries."

In the United States, geographic diversity often refers to a generalization based on class, status, race, ethnicity, or other differences that exist among people. Particularly, the strong ties between status and neighborhood make geographic diversity known to people who identify places using stereotypes. Examples are those big states and regions in the country with large populations and diverse ethnic backgrounds. Regions and states which are subject to national stereotypes are the South, West, Midwest, New England, Florida, Texas, New York, and California (Heuberger, 2001).

Diversity Education

People often feel nervous, tense, or uncomfortable when they hear something is going on about diversity in their workplaces. In the past two decades diversity education has become a grave concern of the leadership teams of major organizations including but not limited to educational institutions. These feelings and tensions are generated from a lack of education about diversity in our society. The key principals that are emphasized by many experts in the field are **awareness** and **understanding**. These two primary requirements in any multicultural setting provide individuals with the necessary vision to look at the world with acceptance and respect (see appendix A: Why Diversity Training Still Matters?, by Carole Copeland Thomas).

Awareness is a sense of gathering information about someone or something. To begin with one needs to have a good self-awareness. Self-awareness is an effective tool in diversity education, and should be experienced along with understanding other peoples' ideas, beliefs, traditions, and sensitivities. Understanding differences is a challenge for most people who have never been around people different from themselves. For example, a former student of mine from a rural area of Wisconsin, who had never seen anybody different from his own ethnicity found it quite challenging when life brought him to a major metropolitan area for higher education where he interacted with many diverse people. Understanding diversity is not an easy task. Wise families can help prepare children prior to facing a bigger world.

Cultural Diversity Education Should Begin at Home

John Locke, an English philosopher, in his work, *An Essay Concerning Human Understanding* (1690), expressed his view that humans everywhere are born as "empty cabinets" and that by filling the cabinets with different experiences, they change who they are (Middleton, 2003). Starting with this analogy of John Locke, I would like to express that parents and the environment of each child play important roles in shaping personalities and minds. In other words, the family institution is a remarkable entity that one should graduate from with flying colors. What we are teaching our children today is the basis for what will make things better for them tomorrow.

Imagine how a gardener lovingly tends his garden on a daily basis. Imagine how a loving parent is so excited to raise a child—both take a lot of love, patience and care. Everything can have an impact on a child or a seedling, good or bad. Some people swear by talking to their plants they grow big and healthy. However, there are parents who do not realize what they are doing to their children by talking negatively about others. Unfortunately, they do not teach their children how to accept other human beings who are different from them. Instead, they teach them their biases, prejudices, and ethnocentric beliefs that they have believed their whole lives. The fact of the matter is that people of this nature embed a seedling of hatred in their children's heart and feed them as they grow.

Obviously, a young man or a young woman who were raised by parents with ill thoughts about human diversity will find it hard to associate with people from different backgrounds and ethnicities. Just recently, a student of mine expressed that "It is hard not to be a racist." He explained that he always hears his father talking negatively about other people from different backgrounds, enforcing his biases when they have family gatherings, and he encourages that every American should carry a gun to protect themselves from the immigrants who have invaded our country. The same student at the end of the class told me that he would not be a racist, and that this class had changed his life.

We hear many prejudicial stories similar to the one mentioned above everyday from different students. Part of the problem is that complacency and the sense of individualism in our society contribute to our ignorance of other cultures, other ethnicities, or indigenous people.

The "oneness" of mankind, and the jubilance of human dignity guides us to light, to shine, and direct others to the source of light.

Home is the best place to start educating our children about human diversity. With positive attitudes and open-mindedness children can learn basic knowledge about the sea of human variations. Parents should start thinking about educating their children about the similarities and differences amongst cultures. There are quite a few sources available that not only benefit parents in this endeavor but will help our school systems as well. For instance, *the All of a Kind Family* book series teaches about Jewish family life in early America.

The library has many books about children from different cultures that can be read by parents and children together, including *Harlem: A Poem* by Walter Dean Myers, *Arrow to the Sun: A Pueblo Indian Tale* by Gerald McDermott, and *The Flag of Childhood: Poems from the Middle East* by Naomi Shihab Nye, these all give glimpses of varying cultures.

Public Broadcasting Services (PBS) has a variety of educational videos on cultures, ethnicity, and diversity. An educational organization called *Learning Seeds* provides all kinds of educational videos including the topic of cultural diversity. The following books would also be a good place to begin to introduce our diverse world to our children: *Celebrating Likes & Differences: Fun and Easy Theme Units for Exploring Diversity With Young Children* by Susan Hodges, *A Teacher's Handbook for Cultural Diversity, Families, and the Special Education System: Communication and Empowerment* by Beth S. Harry, and *Common Sense About Uncommon Knowledge: The Knowledge Bases for Diversity* by G. Pritch Smith.

Learning about diversity at home, also means learning about your own diversity. Children should understand about their own cultures, where did their ancestors come from, what are their holidays, special foods, native clothing, occupations etc. What differs a Norwegian from a German or a French from an Irish? How can I be all four at once? What makes us American? We need to learn from ancient cultures and the wisdom they insisted be taught to youngsters acquired from ancestors. Native Americans were adamant about teaching their children the characteristics of their culture (see appendix B). The famous lyrics from *South Pacific* by Rodgers and Hammerstein confirm that we need to start from home (Lafair, 2001). It is worth reading:

You've got to be taught
You've got to be taught to hate and fear
You've got to be taught from year to year
It's got to be drummed in your dear little ear
You've got to be carefully taught
You've got to be taught to be afraid
Of people whose eyes are oddly made
And people whose skin is a different shade
You've got to be carefully taught
You've got to be taught before it's too late
Before you are six or seven or eight
To hate all people your relatives hate
You've got to be taught

This important effort should be followed with an emphasis of embracing diversity in the schools, so that cultural diversity will find a place in the hearts and minds of millions of students around the country. Like many other issues, we seem to have started from the top and ignored the bottom.

Less than two decades ago, major organizations started teaching diversity to their personnel. Today, almost all important organizations in this country have trainings and seminars about diversity. Institutions of higher education are slowly beginning to join this national effort. Some require mandatory courses, some have elective ones, and some have not yet begun to offer cultural diversity courses at all. Secondary education is more or less involved with diversity education, but it is not mandatory in all U.S. schools yet. Fortunately, many students are taking the initiative and starting diversity clubs in their own high schools themselves.

Celebrating Diversity

Media has an important role in showing diversity to the entire world. Media connects cultures and promotes diversity due to the fact that it does not know any boundaries! It travels across and penetrates into the regions and realms.

For many years, National Geographic magazine has brought the characteristics of other ethnicities to American homes. The intention of the magazine is not geared toward academic purposes, yet the presence of it in many homes in the United States and other parts of the world can be educational for all ages. Other means of media are also useful for gaining information about diversity. The television is quite instrumental for matters related to diversity, pop culture, and global education. Some non-profit agencies such as PBS (Public Broadcasting Service) are more dedicated to cultural diversity. Radio broadcasting has a wide-spread effect around the world. Radio Free Europe broadcasts a variety of cultural programs. In the United States, broadcasting organizations such as NPR (National Public Radio), a public-supported radio is an on-the-air university for the arts, humanities, and social sciences. Thousands of other radio stations around the country contribute to the celebration of diversity, in one way or another.

We are not waiting for diversity to happen. It is here. Sooner or later, people will be involved in it one way or the other. The United

States is a multicultural nation. It is a global society. In major metropolitan areas of the Unites States such as San Jose, California; Atlanta, Georgia; Chicago, Illinois; The Twin Cities, Minnesota; Miami, Florida; New York-New Jersey; and Virginia-Maryland-D.C. alone, more than 100 ethnic groups live and work together. These important areas are catalysts of diversity in the nation. The celebration of the Festival of Nations that takes place every year in St. Paul, Minnesota is good evidence of a diverse population in the state of Minnesota. San Jose, Chicago, and several other major areas have similar celebrations every year.

We need to increase our level of acceptance and admit that we are living in a unique society that embraces people from all parts of the world regardless of the color of their skin, race, religion, language, national origin, gender, size, disability, sexual orientation, and ideology. In the 2004 movie *Save the Last Dance,* actress Julia Stiles and Sean Patrick Thomas portray a white ballerina and a black hip-hop dancer involved in an interracial romance that is met with hostility and resistance by his family and their friends. Eventually, everyone comes around to understanding that the important point was that they loved and needed each other, not the color of skin. Native American Chief White Shield Arikara expressed his wisdom in this manner: (Nerburn & Mengelkoch, 1991, p. 88)

> The color of the skin makes no difference. What is good and just for one is good and just for the other, and the Great Spirit made all men brothers. I have a red skin, but my grandfather was a white man. What does it matter? It is not the color of the skin that makes me good or bad.

Although it is hard for some people, it is wonderful to remember this advice: "Turn things that hurt you, into things that help other people." We conclude this section by a quote from Suzie Williams—a national diversity speaker: "Let us celebrate the magnificence of our diversity and evolve beyond where we presently are. This will require courage, boldness, and deep commitment" (Williams, 2001, p. 105).

Summary

Diversity is when so many things are showing in one picture. Diversity is when all people from all walks of life with differences and similarities, with diverse cultures and traditions wishfully work together in order to have common ground free from conflicts. The ecosystem of nature is a good example of diversity; it is formed by a variety and multiformity of living organisms. Humans, members of this ecosystem present a community comprised of so many different cultures, backgrounds, ideas, and ways of life. The types of diversity are numerous. Diversity in styles, economic status, political ideas, geographic locations, and social norms generate challenges that need to be emphasized in numerous multi-cultural environments. We need to embrace diversity with all its challenges and benefits. On-going attention is needed to teach diversity at home, at schools, and work. The effort of educating the public on diversity issues is welcomed in many organizations and educational institutions. The media plays an important role in promoting and celebrating diversity everyday, here in the United States and all over the world.

Test Your Knowledge

Part One: Select the best choice.

Instructions: Place the number next to each statement that is agreeable with your understanding, beliefs, or action.
      1. almost always   2. frequently   3. occasionally
      4. hardly ever   5. almost never

1. _____ When a newcomer comes to my community I try to get acquainted and interact with him/her.
2. _____ At my workplace, I am curious to find out if there are any co-workers from different backgrounds. This will help me to know them and make an impression that they are welcomed.
3. _____ My parents taught me that no matter if people have different skin colors, or speak different languages, they should be respected for who they are.
4. _____ Although I grew up in an area where I saw no other person different from me, I respected people who came from different backgrounds.
5. _____ I think it's a good idea to host an exchange student once in a while.
6. _____ When television shows a report from a different country I try to watch it.
7. _____ Jose Gonzales is my neighbor; should he need any help I would try to do my best to help him.
8. _____ There are some foreign guys at my school. I have no problem talking to them.
9. _____ It is appropriate to get acquainted with a person's background and tradition before jumping to a conclusion.
10. _____ Interactions with people from different religious backgrounds does not bother me.

Part Two: Discussion Questions

1. What does diversity mean to you and your family?
2. Have you ever encountered a situation where diversity was a critical issue?
3. When you realized that diversity is a part of your life, what sense contributed to this understanding and why?

4. As you were growing up, how much instruction did you receive about our diverse world?

5. What kind of media have been informative to your awareness on diversity and why?

6. How do you value diversity?

7. How did you socialize with an opposite gender in your childhood?

8. What was your reaction when you first saw a person with a different skin tone?

"Fortunately, the time has long passed when people liked to regard the United States as some kind of melting pot, taking men and women from every part of the world and converting them into standardized, homogenized Americans. We are, I think, much more mature and wise today. Just as we welcome a world of diversity, so we glory in an America of diversity — an America all the richer for the many different and distinctive strands of which it is woven."

-Vice President Hubert H. Humphrey

"Mankind will endure when the world appreciates the logic of diversity."

-Indira Gandhi
Prime Minister of India, 1966-77 and 1980-84

"We all should know that diversity makes for a rich tapestry, and we must understand that all the threads of tapestry are equal in value no matter what their color."

-Maya Angelou
American Poet

Chapter 3: From Melting Pot to a Multicultural Society

"The task that remains is to cope with our interdependence—to see ourselves reflected in every other human being and to respect and honor our differences."

-Melba Pattillo Beals
Civil Rights Activist

Objectives

- Identify the difference between the melting pot and multiculturalism
- Distinguish the functions of assimilation, acculturation and enculturation
- Explore the characteristics of different ethnicities in America
- Discuss the important issues in a multicultural society
- Recognize the virtual community within the global society

The Melting Pot

It is hard to clear the term "melting pot" from the minds of Americans and many people from all over the world. "Throughout much of the nation's history the majority of its people subscribed to the melting pot ideology. It was taught in schools, reflected in our literature and disseminated through the media" (Boyd, 1997). This term was coined from the early stages of American history. The analogy of melting pot refers to the period when Anglo-Europeans swarmed this land of opportunity, followed by Asians, and other ethnicities that one by one settled and made it their home. Needless to say, the settlers occupied the land of indigenous people through numerous battles. When the English established their language and heritage to be the main elements of the social fabric in America they generated **Eurocentrism**, the practice of consciously or unconsciously privileging the culture of Europe over other cultures. With the same token, prejudice that centralizes one's ethnicity and puts other ethnicities in the periphery is called "**ethnocentrism**." In other words, it is a practice or belief of unconsciously or consciously privileging a certain ethnic group over others, simply, judging other groups by the values of one's own group. Ostensibly, other cultures resembling no compatibility to the Anglo-European norms and standards were considered as sub-standard.

It was hard for some Europeans, even Irish people to be accepted as part of society. History reveals that many adapted to the environment and adopted the main stream culture that the English structured. To this date, there are some Americans who retained little or no features of their heritage and language and became all American. This is the best example of assimilation. **Assimilation,** therefore, is a product of the melting pot, referring to the process whereby a minority group gradually adopts the customs and attitudes of the majority. As America was shaping through slavery, confederation battles, democracy, industrialization, and finally unity, the melting pot analogy became a myth rather than a fact. Some people were not allowed to assimilate, some did not want to join the majority and chose to retain their culture and heritage (Sonnenschein, 1997). Therefore, "melting pot" remains to be a myth. Lindsey and Beach (2002) explain this quite well:

> For most of the twentieth century, the dominant image was of America as a melting pot—a giant cauldron where people of diverse backgrounds would be submerged and then reemerge as a unified group known as "Americans." In this hypothetical melting pot, immigrants would shed previous cultural identities and embrace the culture and values of their new homeland. This ideal held sway, although it was never fully achieved in practice. Some ethnic groups were not considered 100 percent American—whether they were deliberately and forcibly excluded from main stream society (especially African Americans and Native Americans), or chose to maintain their distinctive ethnic identity (Latinos, to some degree Italian Americans, as well as groups such

as the Mormons and Amish), or a combination of
the two (p.77).

Multiculturalism

In May 1607, an English settlement was founded in
Jamestown, a village in South East Virginia. Africans came to the
United States against their will starting with the first slave ship in
1619. Other European immigrants, either voluntarily or compellingly,
left their homelands and entered the United States in the 17th century.

When the Chinese started arriving at the western shores of
America more than one hundred and fifty years before the Europeans
showed up, they experienced no disturbance from any other culture.
The first intolerance of a different culture appeared in 1882 with the
issuance of the Chinese Exclusion Act, generating the first law
prohibiting the entry of immigrants on the basis of nationality (Takaki,
1996).

American society, with the help of democracy, freedom, and
justice for all, has come a long way towards accepting and respecting
people residing in all 50 states—citizens and immigrants—who
represented themselves with various cultures, ethnicities, races,
religions, as well as ideas and opinions. The fact is, that today the
world is comprised of 192 countries (National Geographic, 2002) or
independent states. It should be noted that 202 countries or
independent states participated in the 2004 Summer Olympics in
Athens, Greece. At least 15 percent of these countries have welcomed
multiculturalism. Among them, the most prominent are the United
States, Canada, England, Australia, New Zealand, China, and other
cosmopolitan states in Europe, the Middle East, Asia, Africa, and
Latin America, to name a few. Accordingly, **multiculturalism** is the
practice of acknowledging and respecting the various cultures,
religions, races, ethnicities, attitudes and opinions within an
environment. It is therefore, appropriate to say that the "melting pot" is
a myth and "multiculturalism" is a fact. Growing diversity has been
emphasized by many researchers for the last 30 years or so. The
demographer Harold Hodgkinson, on the expansion and growth of
diversity and multiculturalism tells us that: In the 1960 census two
categories were identified, black and white. By the 1990 census there
were more than 40 racial and ethnic groups recorded (Calvin, 2001).
The year 2000 census recorded 80 racial and ethnic groups (The U.S.

Census Bureau, 2004). Before the census 2010 we shall see at least 10 more racial and ethnic groups added to the previous recording in the United States. This has already been observed in Minnesota and other multicultural states (Star Tribune, 2001).

In the midst of multiculturalism, when an individual, group, or people retain more of their background while adapting the main stream culture, the phenomenon of **Acculturation** comes to play which means: cultural modification of an individual, group, or people by adapting to or borrowing traits from another culture; a merging of cultures as a result of prolonged contact. According to Garcia (2002) acculturation refers to the process by which the members of a society learn and act upon a society's main culture. There are quite a few examples of this process in multicultural societies. In the United States, immigrants from many parts of the world with different ethnic backgrounds learn the main stream culture and act upon it, although they retain much of their cultures. "The acculturation process is a crucial consideration in the analysis of ethnic minorities in pluralistic societies" (Garcia, 2002: p. 79).

Immigrants and our Perception

Immigration has always been a controversial issue in the United States. In recent years, especially after September 11, and during the election year of 2004, talk about immigration increased. There are so many myths about illegal immigration, yet we should bear in mind that for every myth there may be indeed a fact. Conventional wisdom seeks the fact and throws away the myth. With the flux of immigrants comes cultural diversity and for many, confusion and misperceptions.

Alex Boyd (1997), in the *Guide to Multicultural Resources* reminds us that "well over one hundred identifiable ethnic groups currently live in the United States, and over 130 languages and dialects are spoken." Looking at the mid-central United States, for example, Minnesota, there are at least 99 ethnic groups represented and the majority of them reside in the greater Twin Cities (Minneapolis-St. Paul). The major ethnic groups who came to Minnesota in recent years include Hispanic, Hmong, Somalis, Vietnamese, and Russians.

Myths and Facts

There so many myths and facts about immigrants these days. For example, a myth says that: "Most immigrants to the United States are illegal, undocumented aliens who come only for economic reasons." The fact is: based on INS records, 849,807 immigrants were legally admitted to our country in the year 2000. The fact of the matter is that economics played a role in these arrivals, but more importantly family, secured jobs, and freedom, in particular, are significant elements and factors that influenced these people's decision to leave their homeland. The majority of Americans can not understand how difficult it is to leave your birthplace, relatives, friends, culture, and the accustomed environment and flee to a country where you have to start from scratch, bear strange looks and some animosity, accept low-paying jobs, and be deprived from the many amenities of life that are readily available for others. According to recent data, among the immigrants who came to this country in 2000, 69% arrived to be reunited with their immediate family members, 13% came to fill the jobs no U.S. worker was willing or available to do, and 8% were refugees who fled their countries due to persecution and found the U.S. as a land of safety and freedom. Like generations of immigrants before them, these immigrants came to this country looking for a better life, and their energy and ideas enrich all our communities.

Listening to Immigrants (An Experience in Minnesota)

According to a demographic profile of the Census Information 2000 obtained from Startribune.com, a significant number of foreign born, and especially the Hispanic population (about 4000) are scattered in Carver and Scott counties. Chaska, and Shakopee have the highest number of the Hispanic population. Some Somalis, out of 15,000 who reside in the Twin Cities live in or around this community. A large group of Russians also settled in Shakopee.

The Commissioners of Human Rights in Chaska have volunteered their time, energy, and expertise to make sure no human rights are violated, and that these rights are protected and respected. Their next duty is to educate the public about community values, historical heritage, and social interactions.

Experiencing the cultural diversity in these small communities encourages human rights advocates to make sure immigrants are welcomed and have the opportunity to make a happy life in their new habitat. Suggestions and recommendations from all ethnic groups in the community are welcomed and new immigrants are invited to contact authorities if they have questions or concerns. Human rights advocates listen to immigrants and take notes of all requests. After careful review, the Commission will take action on the legitimate ones. For example, in one of the sessions, the Hispanic population requested that the city should provide written communications in Spanish and distribute them in local stores so those who have no command of the English language can understand the basic requirements of daily life, especially during the period of adjusting to the environment and learning the language of the main stream culture.

Blending with the Mainstream

Today, men and women from different backgrounds and national origins who come to the United States plant the seeds of hope in their hearts and minds that they are considered part of the American community. In this respect, they make their genuine effort to blend with mainstream America by improving their English, the legal language of the land, in order to accommodate their basic needs. Early immigrants who came to this country from all parts of Europe and Asia assimilated themselves to mainstream America. This land of freedom and opportunity respects all religions, languages, ideas, and traditions. We acknowledge cultural diversity and appreciate traditions of other lands, arts, food, etc.—in fact, we welcome them!

To this day some may ask: Who is an American? What criteria a person should have to be called an American? Is it enough to be born in the U.S. to be considered an American? Or, is someone an American when he or she gains the U.S. citizenship? The answers to these questions are embedded in multiculturalism and the following famous letter of an Australian dentist to the world answers many questions:

An Australian's thoughts of Americans:

An e-mail sent to millions around the world as a public domain

In 2003, there was a report that someone in Pakistan had published in a newspaper an offer of a reward to anyone who killed an

American, any American. So an Australian dentist wrote the following to let everyone know what an American is, so they would know when they found one!

"An American is English, or French, or Italian, Irish, German, Spanish, Polish, Russian or Greek. An American may also be Canadian, Mexican, African, Indian, Chinese, Japanese, Australian, Iranian, Asian, or Arab, or Pakistani, or Afghan. An American may also be a Cherokee, Osage, Blackfoot, Navaho, Apache, or one of the many other tribes known as Native Americans.

An American is Christian, or he could be Jewish, or Buddhist, or Muslim. In fact, [there are more Muslims in America than in Afghanistan]. The only difference is that in America they are free to worship as each of them chooses. An American is also free to believe in no religion. For that he will answer only to God, not to the government, or to armed thugs claiming to speak for the government and for God.

An American is from the most prosperous land in the history of the world. The root of that prosperity can be found in the Declaration of Independence, which recognizes the God given right of each man and woman to the pursuit of happiness. An American is generous. Americans have helped out just about every other nation in the world in their time of need. When Afghanistan was overrun by the Soviet army 20 years ago, Americans came with arms and supplies to enable the people to win back their country. As of the morning of September 11, Americans had given more than any other nation to the poor in Afghanistan.

Americans welcome the best, the best products, the best books, the best music, the best food, the best athletes. But they also welcome the least. The national symbol of America, the Statue of Liberty, welcomes your tired and your poor, the wretched refuse of your teeming shores, the homeless, tempest tossed. These in fact are the people who built America. Some of them were working in the Twin Towers the morning of September 11, earning a better life for their families. I've been told that the World Trade Center victims were from at least 30 other countries, cultures, and first languages, including those that aided and abetted the terrorists.

So you can try to kill an American if you must. Hitler did. So did General Tojo, and Stalin, and Mao Tse-Tung, and every bloodthirsty tyrant in the history of the world. But, in doing so you would just be killing yourself. Because Americans are not a particular people from a particular place. They are the embodiment of the human spirit of freedom. Everyone who holds to that spirit, everywhere, is an American."

A Celebration of Cultures

Today, the United States is considered a multiracial nation. Takaki (1996), referring to Rodney King's tragedy on April 22, 1992 in Los Angeles, argues that "One of the lessons of the Los Angeles explosion is the recognition of the fact that we are a multiracial society and that race can no longer be defined in the binary terms of white and black." (p.5) It is fervently appropriate to include Asians, Hispanics, and other races that, too, shape the American societal fabric. Multiculturalism is not a special practice that has occurred only in the United States, it is pragmatic in many parts of the world such as Canada, Australia, England, France, Italy, Spain, Brazil, and other democratic societies that embrace people from all backgrounds without the harsh prejudice and discrimination carried out in many countries—even in the 21st century.

When immigrants in the United States are granted citizenship by the Immigration and Naturalization Services (INS), the federal judge congratulates them for becoming bona fide American citizens. The judge also recommends that they should not forget where they came from and urges that they should celebrate their cultures and ethnic background. It is a great idea that people should learn about their cultures and celebrate their heritage. Learning about your own culture is called **enculturation**. In other words, enculturation is a learning outcome that indicates who you are and what cultural heritage you belong to. A good example of enculturation is the creation of Kwanzaa by Dr. Maulana Karenga in 1966. Karenga is famous for creating this African American and Pan-African holiday to promote the communitarian African philosophy. He came up with this idea to help Africans learn more about their historical significance and heritage hallmarks, and more importantly teach their children to remember their African genesis. **Kwanzaa** is a seven-day cultural celebration of African Americans which begins on December 26 and ends on January 1. The meaning of Kwanzaa is "the first fruit" which was based upon the Seven Principles (*Nguzo Saba)*: 1) *umoja*: unity, 2) *kujichagulia*: self-determination, 3) *ujima*: collective works and responsibilities, 4) *ujamaa*: cooperative economics, 5): *nia*: purpose, 6) *kuumba:* creativity, and 7) *imani*: faith (Asante, 2002; Heuberger, 2001). The opportunity to learn about African heritage and other ethnic groups should be available in all levels of education. Cultural diversity education in college fills the gap of the necessary cultural education that was neglected in the secondary education system.

Throughout the United States, you may find many places that value cultural heritage and the uniqueness of ethnicities by organizing annual festivals, tastes of cultures, and celebrations of diversity. In major areas such as Chicago, New York, Los Angeles, Miami, Minneapolis-St. Paul, and San Diego, to name a few, thousands of cultural appreciators participate to pay tribute and compliment different ethnicities every year. The Festival of Nations, for example, in St. Paul, Minnesota, is a remarkable celebration of cultures. This fabulous event has been going on since 1932 and is sponsored by the International Institute of Minnesota. The Festival features more than 90 ethnic groups who present delicious food, spectacular dance performances, creative folk arts, and fascinating cultural show rooms. Also, the Minneapolis Mosaic, a 6-week celebration of ethnicity through the arts, takes place every year in early summer through multiple events which add tremendously to the creativity and innovation of cultural diversity.

Summary

Many do not distinguish the difference between the "melting pot" and "multiculturalism." Although we have formed a global society in the United States, the general public still thinks of America as the world's melting pot. The fact of the matter is that the analogy of the melting pot did not work and remained a myth. In the early stages of American history, some were not allowed to assimilate, and some did not want to join the majority of predominantly white Anglo-Saxons. Even the Irish had difficulty blending with the English. Consequently, African-Americans, who were brought to the United States against their will, the Native-Americans who were here originally, and other minority groups maintained their heritage while growing up with the system that gradually formed this multi-racial society. As a result, multiculturalism was born and evolved throughout the 20th century. We are all Americans—no matter what backgrounds we have. We are all Americans—no matter what color we are—or how we look. Today, in the United States, Canada, Australia, France, England and other parts of the world, people from different races, ethnicity, religion, and ideology live and work together with the hope that they can get along together with their existing differences. Cultural diversity becomes a more and more important matter for societies such as ours, primarily because humanity should be praised and valued regardless of differences. We need to embrace our differences, fill the gap with awareness, understanding and acceptance, and cherish our similarities.

Test Your Knowledge

Part One: Select the best choice.

Instruction: In front of each statement below put "E" for ethnocentric, or "R" for reality.

_____1 The Anglo-European culture tended to be superior and non-Europeans received no credit for what they did to form the American nation.

_____2 Europeans are more civilized than other cultures.

_____3 Buddhism is largely practiced in East and Southeast Asia.

_____4 The system of education in the United States is superior to those of other nations.

_____5 People around the world should learn from Judaism, the 4,000-year-old religion of the Jews, that teaches the best way how to raise a child.

_____6 Americans have helped out just about every other nation in the world in their time of need.

_____7 The largest producer of caviar in the world is the Caspian Sea region.

_____8 North African food is the most tasteful comparing to other international cuisine.

_____9 The growth of Islam and the decline of the traditional Chinese religion stand out as significant changes over the past hundred years.

_____10 The French tradition of hospitality, by far, is the best in the world.

_____11 All major religions originated in Asia.

_____12 Jazz and Blues, are authentic in the United States.

Part Two: Discussion Questions

1. Why can the challenge of cultural diversity no longer be ignored?
2. The predominant privileged white citizens in the United States are mostly under fire for discrimination and other challenges of diversity. What is your reaction to this sentiment?
3. What should be our position today since Native Americans, African Americans, and non-Europeans were not treated appropriately in the past by our ancestors?

4. Should the United States be lenient towards immigration laws or do we need to be more stringent about people wanting to immigrate to our country?

5. In the next century or so, Hispanic, African Americans, and Asian Americans will outnumber the Caucasian population. How will this impact the economy and social norms in the United States?

6. To what extent should "Kwanzaa" be taught in U.S. schools?

"Prejudice is learned. It's not a self-winding watch."

-Muhammad Ali

"Working with children is the easiest part of educating for democracy, because children are still undefeated and have no stake in being prejudiced."
-Margaret Halsey
American novelist

"Those who will not reason, are bigots, those who cannot, are fools, and those who dare not, are slaves."

-Lord Byron
English poet *(1788-1824)*

Part Two
Our Social Interactions

Chapter 4: Diversity and Reactive Syndromes

"Prejudice is a burden which confuses the past, threatens the future, and renders the present inaccessible."

-Maya Angelou
American poet and author

Objectives

- Explore the cause of reaction vis-à-vis diversity
- Define stereotype
- Recognize different types of stereotyping
- Identify prejudice, bias, and bigotry
- Comprehend the use of critical thinking for problem solving
- Distinguish denigration and defamation of character
- Exemplify the ramification of negative thinking
- Analyze the root of hate crime and legal protection

Introduction

According to the third Newtonian law for every action there is a reaction. This has been observed in nature and the human environment. When we think about it in a psychological way we tend to rekindle our observation and seek a manner that is normal for a regular human being. We react to so many things in our lives, yet for every matter we may pose certain responses that could create a situation that is not ordinary to the majority of people. In diversity, where issues are extraordinarily sensitive, these reactions may create a hurtful circumstance, an intense situation, be uneasy to deal with, possibly unpleasant to many, or inevitably, a syndrome. Subsequently, those reactions that create tension, hard feelings, and sometimes humiliation are called "reactive syndrome." Reactive syndromes happen in the work place, in public, or anywhere that is hosting a variety of people from different backgrounds. The following types of reactive syndrome are the most common cause of unjust consideration in human diversity. These are not new to human life and they are not going to go away easily unless we learn how to reconsider our behaviors reasonably and thoughtfully for the sake of tenderness, sensitivity, and peace of mind.

Stereotype

Often times in conversation people express themselves without certainty and truthful observation. Stating generalizations and making assumptions about something, someone, or a group of people is called stereotype. One should not make a judgment based on some observations or factual recollection, and assume that he or she is stating a fact. Stereotypes can be positive or negative. For example, saying "all people in America are rich," although not true, is a positive stereotype, yet does not make anybody upset. Conversely, statements such as "all people in Mexico are poor" or "people from southern states of the U.S. are bigots" are negative stereotypes and unrealistic which may bother some people. Negative stereotypes generating from a misunderstanding or lack of knowledge about people who are different from us causes arguments, harsh situations, and sometimes animosity. It has become an essential point in diversity trainings to educate people about stereotyping as the first reactive syndrome while addressing the challenges of diversity that separate us from each other.

Prejudice

Prejudice is a judgment or opinion formed before the facts are known. In other words, prejudice is defined as when we have a preconceived idea about something or someone, either favorable, or more usually, unfavorable. For example, holding an irrational judgment or opinion about a certain individual or a group of people is considered a prejudice.

Prejudice is synonymous with bigotry. It is of possessing a narrow-minded attitude or behavior which includes, but not limited to, being judgmental, intolerant, or hating other races, creeds, national origins, geographic regions, religions, occupations, and ideology, to name a few. In diversity, prejudice is a key element of ignorance and segregation. For example, in the civil rights movement of 1954 to

1965 prejudicial reactions brought injurious results and the loss of lives to the black population and white supporters in the United States.

Critical Thinking

Although critical thinking is vastly used in general science, in cultural diversity it is particularly used to lower the level of prejudice. As an effective tool, critical thinking has been used by social scientists for problem solving. Prior to finding the benefits of critical thinking for problem solving it is necessary to state the definition first. Critical thinking is an intellectual skill used by many who wish to study something—particularly subjects of behavioral sciences. By asking good questions, especially open-ended questions, one should inspect whether the evidence supports the conclusions and provide suggestions of alternative interpretations. Other aspects of critical thinking are comprised of the investigation of any potential biases and the exploration of whether or not conclusions have been over-generalized or over-simplified. Finally, it is important to check the obstacles that may confront critical thinking. These hindrances could be incomplete comparisons, biased language, inclination towards the idea's popularity, and individuals preference for certainty. (Matlin, 1999)

In short, critical thinking skills help us reduce prejudice. These skills are a good use of language, testing for inferences, recognizing assumptions, reasoning, analyzing arguments, seeking evidence, and formulating conclusions. While people can not often control their feelings, they can control their thoughts and behavior. The most important critical thinking dispositions that are used in reducing the level of prejudice are: open-mindedness, respect for other view points, objectivity, intellectual curiosity, flexibility, intellectual honesty, persistence, being systematic, and decisiveness.

Bigotry

Whatever is associated with prejudice can be related to bigotry as well. Bigotry, in general, can be defined as intolerance or prejudice. It is indeed the behavior, attitude, or beliefs of a bigot. A bigot is a person who holds blindly and intolerantly to a particular creed, opinion or belief. According to the Webster's Dictionary (Guralnik, 1986, p. 139), "a bigot is a narrow-minded person."

A recent episode of the TV show "Strong Medicine" on the Lifetime Television for Women channel portrayed a white woman going to meet the parents of her black boyfriend. His mother was prejudiced against the girlfriend not only for being white, but his mother also didn't think that the white woman was of their "class" or good enough for her black son. By the end of the show, they reconciled and his mother accepted her. The mother realized how wrong she was to be prejudiced.

Bias

The training guide for hate crime data collection prepared by the U.S. Department of Justice (DOJ, 1996), defines bias as "a performed negative opinion or attitude toward a group of persons based on their race, religion, disability, ethnicity/national origin, or sexual orientation." Simply, when we judge something or someone and include our personal feelings or attachment in it we incur a bias. A "bias implies a mental leaning in favor of or against someone or something" (Guralnik, 1986, p. 1122). In other words, justification with no string attached to it is an unbiased validation of something or someone. For example, a judge can not be a judge if he or she practices with a biased opinion; a teacher on evaluation of a student should not include any kind of biases, and a person who reviews an article for publication does his/her job with no bias. Bias is a synonym to predilection, which implies a preconceived liking, formed as a result of one's background, or temperament.

Denigration

Talking negatively behind friends, colleagues, or relatives in a way that defame their characters is considered denigration. Originally, the word "denigrate" means blacken. To blacken someone's reputation, or defamation of character is what we perceive as denigration. Denigration more often occurs in the workplace. In a diverse workplace some people create a hostile environment by denigrating other colleagues. A more debilitating situation is when an immature and unsophisticated manger or supervisor talks behind his or her employee's back. Simply, the act of disparaging the character or reputation of a person or a group of people is known as denigration. In the realm of diversity, defamation of people of Jewish faith and other religious beliefs is seriously condemned. The ADL (Anti Defamation League) is a prestigious organization that provides educational resources nationwide to millions of people about denigration and defamation.

Hate Crimes

Hate crimes are not a new phenomenon. Human history has recorded many incidents that have been linked with hatred and bigotry for many decades. Focusing on the United States, hate crimes originated from the early history of our nation.

Let's begin with defining "hate" and "crime" first. Hate, according to most dictionaries is defined as: *intense dislike and animosity, or: to feel animosity or hostility toward*; then we have related words such as hateful, hatred and so forth. Crime, on the other hand, is defined as: an *act committed or omitted in violation of a law forbidding or commanding it and for which punishment is imposed upon conviction*, or *unlawful activity, an unjust, senseless, or disgraceful act or condition*. With these simple definitions we can have a better understanding of "hate-crime" that is, *an unlawful act that is committed based on intensive animosity*. This is a criminal act that is predominantly based on "differences," or diversification which is related to color, race, gender, nation of origin, culture, religion, language, physical disabilities, sexual orientation, ideology, and occupation to name a few.

Hate crimes have been observed throughout the history of mankind everywhere in the world. In our history of modern time, hate crimes in the United States stem from slavery, racial injustice, and prejudice against blacks in the era of the civil rights movement, and continued by spreading into the society where it was permeated by harming the uniqueness of diverse people. In recent years, hate crimes have been particularly synonymous with the gay and lesbian population. Bigotry against homosexual citizens has caused many shameful crimes around the country.

In 1998, Mathew Shepard, a 21-year-old gay college student was tied to a fence pole, beaten, and left to die in the middle of a field in a Wyoming farmland. He died five days later. For further information on Mathew Shepard you may refer to: (http://www.matthewshepard.org/) and (http://www.geocities.com/WestHollywood/Stonewall/2878/).

The case of Mathew Shepard will not ever be forgotten. In November 26, 2004, an investigation by ABC's 20/20 put forth the theory that Mathew Shepard's murder was not a hate crime, but a drug-related robbery gone wrong. However, this theory has not been validated or corroborated at the time of this printing, so we shall continue to consider this an example of heinous hate crime for the time being.

Even more recent and subtle examples are the incidents that occurred after September 11. The lack of understanding, generalizing, and assuming intertwined with anger and animosity decimated many innocent lives around the country that had no connection with the tragedy of 9/11.

Why do People Commit Hate Crimes?

Some experts believe that hate crimes have psychological connections. It starts with behavioral problems, develops with antisocial activities, and could end with terrorism, homicide, genocide, or other debilitating crimes. Although you have seen many kinds of crimes associated with hate, bias, or bigotry in the past, the term "hate crime" is a product of the mid 1990s. Antisocial (psychopathic) personality is a personal disorder. Those individuals who possess psychopathic personalities are "basically dissociated and evidently incapable of significant loyalty to other persons, groups, or social values." Primarily, the lack of awareness of socialization in a person's life might be the breeding ground for hate crimes. Furthermore, we need to look at what influenced these individuals as they were growing up and what continues to influence them today. According to diversity experts, typical influences include family, personal experiences, education, friends, the media, and critical incidents or events. For example, if we pick up a pretext such as "gender" the question would be: What influenced an individual as a child and adolescent to describe, interpret, and evaluate their gender? That is to say, family institutions, the media, and special interest groups are for the most part responsible for problems such as the hate crimes that we see in our society. A message from the Minnesota Attorney General's Office elaborates our point: "These crimes tear apart the fabric of our communities. They are intended to intimidate all those like the victim, to tell them that they and their kind are not welcome here."

Education, Prevention, Response

Just recently, one of the afternoon radio talk show hosts was debating about 9/11 with one of his listening audience: he argued that "the Nine-Eleven tragedy was not a hate crime." Wrong! The

September 11 tragedy was definitely a hate crime. It was a horrible criminal act and it was full of hatred towards American society and its way of life. It was a horrible, inhumane, and unforgettable slaughter of more than 3000 innocent civilians by a group of Islamic fundamentalists who hated our democracy, our freedom, our religion, our modernization, our ideology, our respect for women, and above all our supreme power. Terrorism is a product of hate that can be committed by any person, domestic or from outside.

We need to educate our children, the generations of tomorrow, to eliminate this predicament from our society. We need to mobilize our resources and educate people to receive help from respective authorities immediately before it is too late. It was announced earlier that the prevention of hate crimes starts in schools, churches and neighborhoods. Consequently, several communities have begun to form hate crime networks in many states around the country. Many volunteers associated with Hate Crime Response and Prevention Networks around the U.S. spend unlimited time and effort to minimize hate crimes around the country. The most immediate public service announcement of these organizations is to encourage hate crime victims to report incidents to local law enforcement authorities with no delay. A report from the State of Minnesota, Department of Public Safety, for example, reveals that there were 209 records of biased offenses from January through December 2001, which indicates a 14% increase over the year 2000. Among biased offenses, racial and sexual orientation were the highest incidences.

Hate and Bias-Motivated Crime Resources

As long as we have bigots, prejudice, and psychopathic personalities, hate crimes can happen—at work, at your residence, in parking lots, in public places, and everywhere else. No time should be wasted. If a hate crime happens in your neighborhood, you should report it to the police right away. Contact your local Human Rights Commission or the following agencies for immediate assistance: your local FBI office, your local Department of Human Rights, your local NAACP chapter, your local Anti Defamation League, your local Jewish Community Relations Council, your local Urban League, and your local Gay and Lesbian Community Action Council, if any. Although many communities in the United States may not have experienced hate crimes, nevertheless we need to be prepared. This can happen anywhere, at anytime. Even in the middle of a field in Wyoming.

Hate Crime Legislation

In recent years, people, local authorities, and states agencies that deal with hate crime-related incidents have forced the federal government to do something about it. The following events provide important information about hate crimes prevention measures in the United States:

Current Legislation

Since 1990, there have been several legislative moves addressing hate crimes: (www.racerelations.about.com, 2005)

o   The Hate Crimes Statistics Act of 1990
o   Violence Against Women Act of 1994
o   Hate Crimes Sentencing Enhancement Act
o   Church Arsons Prevention Act of 1996
o   Hate Crimes Prevention Act of 1998
o   The Violence Against Women Act of 1998
o   Hate Crimes Prevention Act of 1999
o   The Federal Hate Crime Laws, 2004

In addition, 42 states have hate crimes laws in effect, 21 of which include legislation against acts of violence based on sexual orientation.

*   **1990:** The Hate Crime Statistics Act was a ground breaking national effort. In this Act, hate crimes are defined as "...crimes that manifest evidence of prejudice based on race, religion, sexual orientation, or ethnicity, including where appropriate the crimes of murder, non-negligent manslaughter, forcible rape, aggravated assault, simple assault, intimidation, arson, and destruction, damage or vandalism of property." (DOJ, 1996: 5)
*   **1994:** The definition of hate crimes was modified in the federal 1994 Hate Crimes Sentencing Enhancement Act as "...crimes in which the defendant intentionally selects a victim, or in the case of a property crime, the property that is the object of the crime, because of the actual or perceived race, color, religion,

national origin, ethnicity, gender, disability or sexual orientation of any person."

The hate crime law was a major federal crime bill, and allowed for increasing sentences for crimes that are proven to be hate crimes and applies only to crimes committed on federal premises.

- **1999:** The Federal Hate Crimes Prevention Act was introduced and passed by the Senate, but did not pass the House of Representatives.
- **2004:** On June 15, 2004, the U.S. Senate overwhelmingly (65 to 33 votes) passed the Hate Crime Prevention Law. This ensures full prosecution of hate crimes in the United States.

Summary

In the realm of diversity, differences create misunderstandings; misunderstandings generate discomfort; and discomfort causes reactions that in the worst case scenario, the price is so heavy, sometimes resulting in the loss of lives. The factors that stimulate tension, animosity, and often a devastating outcome are called reactive syndromes. Starting from stereotypes, bigotry, bias, and ending with denigration and hate crimes, diversity encounters a variety of phenomena that makes life uneasy for most people. In the United States of America, where so many racial groups live and work together it is beneficial to know about reactive syndromes and become familiar with their consequences should one need to take precautionary measures and know effective ways to prevent them.

Most discrimination in the world is caused by stereotypes, prejudice, bigotry, bias, denigration, and hatred. The reasons why we have these syndromes can be found in the thoughts, communication, and behavior of individuals. Unfortunately, incidents happen when people do not have enough knowledge about other people or places or misunderstand circumstances and situations. Within this mind-boggling plethora one who is not color blind, one who does not believe in integration, one who possesses cultural supremacy over others, one who selects hatred to be the focus of their lives, and one who persuades defamation of character and reputation will have difficulty working and living with others as we have already entered a world of diversity and inclusion.

Quotes from Coretta Scott King, 1927-2006

The widow of Martin Luther King, Jr., she was a civil rights activist and carried on the work of her husband while raising 4 children. She died on January 31, 2006.

·   *"Hate is too great a burden to bear. It injures the hater more than it injures the hated."*

·   *"I believe all Americans who believe in freedom, tolerance and human rights have a responsibility to oppose bigotry and prejudice based on sexual orientation."*

·   *"I'm fulfilled in what I do ... I never thought that a lot of money or fine clothes—the finer things of life—would make you happy. My concept of happiness is to be filled in a spiritual sense."*

·   *"There is a spirit and a need and a man at the beginning of every great human advance. Every one of these must be right for that particular moment of history, or nothing happens."*

·   *"Women, if the soul of the nation is to be saved, I believe that you must become its soul."*

·   *"Segregation was wrong when it was forced by white people, and I believe it is still wrong when it is requested by black people."*

·   *"Struggle is a never-ending process. Freedom is never really won; you earn it and win it in every generation."*

·   *"I still hear people say that I should not be talking about the rights of lesbian and gay people and I should stick to the issue of racial justice. But I hasten to remind them that Martin Luther King Jr. said, 'Injustice anywhere is a threat to justice everywhere.' I appeal to everyone who believes in Martin Luther King Jr.'s dream to make room at the table of brother- and sisterhood for lesbian and gay people."*

"If American women would increase their voting turnout by ten percent, I think we would see an end to all of the budget cuts in programs benefiting women and children."

Test Your Knowledge

Part One: Select the best choice.
Instruction: In front of each statement below put "P" for positive stereotype and "N for negative stereotype.
1.____French people are the best cooks in the world.
2.____Asian Americans are excellent workers.
3.____Gays are the best hairstylists.
4.____Southern people in the United States are prejudiced.
5.____Women are the best drivers.
6.____Men are the best financial advisors.
7.____Peoples from warm climates have low IQs.
8.____Blacks in the United States are the best musicians.
9.____The people from the Middle East support terrorism.
10.____Jews are stingy people.
11.____Japanese men cheat on their wives.
12.____Italians are the best lovers.

Part Two: Discussion Questions
1. What are reactive syndromes and why do they create problems in cultural diversity?
2. Why are some people's first impression always negative rather than positive?
3. How can we eliminate prejudice among us?
4. Compare and contrast negative and positive feelings and explain how one acquires such feelings?
5. Which challenges of diversity are produced by prejudice and bigotry?
6. Who is a denigrator and how does he or she choose their targets?
7. What does defamation do to a person or a group of people?
8. What is the difference between "bias" and "prejudice"?
9. What are the contributing factors of hate crimes?
10. Explain why terrorism is a product of hate crime?
11. Explain how harassment might be related to cultural diversity?

WHAT MATTERS *(A song written about Matthew Shepard after his horrible death.)*
by Randi Driscoll

You were the brightest angel heaven had ever seen
you walked in with a story to tell and ten thousand tongues to scream
and you said
doesn't your heart beat the same as mine
haven't I told you a thousand times
isn't the air in my lungs the same air you breathe

so who cares whose arms I'm all wrapped up in
who cares whoes eyes I see myself in
who cares who I dream of
who cares who I love.

Heaven help me for I am lost
what a price my love did cost
but here I am standing strong and I am free
and didn't we share the same sunrise and sleep in the same moonlight
isn't the blood in my veins the same blood you bleed, so...

when I die
and they lay my body down
the peace that I will find is the peace that brings you all around
doesn't my mother cry like everyone
my father grieve for his lonely son
isn't my rainbow a little brighter because...

so who cares whose arms I'm all wrapped up in
who cares whose eyes I see myself in
who cares who I dream of
no it doesn't matter who I dream of
'cause in the end it only matters that I was loved and am loved...love
has no face.

©1999 Randi Driscoll/Swim Swam Swum Songs/BMI
Lyrics reprinted with permission of the artist.

Chapter 5: The Challenges and Benefits of Diversity

"These people who now call for the end of policies to promote equal opportunity say there's been so much progress that no more such efforts are justified. But they fail to recognize that the tap root of racism is almost 400 years long."

-Vice President Al Gore

"Affirmative action is not a perfect remedy, but it beats the alternative, if the only alternative is to do nothing."

-Clarence Page
Chicago Tribune Columnist

Objectives

- Identify the challenges of diversity
- Recognize the benefits of diversity
- Discuss the important diversity issues in the workplace
- Analyze the national issues of diversity
- Explore the resources in your community to value diversity
- Epitomize the ways of success in a diverse environment

Challenges of Diversity

Before the Americas became acquainted with slavery, the world was already familiar with the concept for a long time. Many ancient countries owned slaves, mainly from Africa, among them specifically, Egyptians, Greeks, and Persians, whose magnificent pyramids, citadels, and palaces could have not been erected without the arduous labor of slaves.

History reveals that the English created the concept of 'black laborers' which led to slavery in America (Middleton, 2003). In 1619, when the first ship carrying Africans approached the shores of the United States, the genesis of diversity challenges emerged. The history of the Civil Rights Movement and the chronology of events that were briefly mentioned before exemplify how minorities were treated by the Anglo-European dominant population. During the nineteenth century, the political storm over slavery almost destroyed the nation (Takaki, 1993).

Even after Abraham Lincoln put an end to slavery, the black population in the United States were not free from the consequences of slavery. African Americans suffered the most due to diverse ethnicity and skin color. The nation should be grateful to Dr. Martin Luther King and other black leaders who peacefully fought for justice and equality in America.

Since the 1950s, the quest for recognition has been quite prominent through many humanitarian and civil liberty organizations. Organizations such as the National Association for the Advancement of Colored People (NAACP), the Anti Defamation League (ADL), the Urban League, American Civil Liberties Union (ACLU), the National Organization for the Advancement of Hispanics (NOAH), and the Asia Pacific Center for Justice and Peace have contributed towards the positive understanding of diversity. According to Kwiesi Mfume, the past president of NAACP, this organization has 1700 chapters around the country and abroad. Today, this organization does not only advocate African American issues, it spreads its wings over all people from a variety of ethnicities.

Diversity of all sorts creates challenges. If people wouldn't discriminate against each other, there would be no significant challenges due to differences. The main attribute that creates challenges is discrimination which happens through racism, sexism, ageism, classism, ableism, and homophobia, to name a few. In today's workplaces, diversity is an important subject for management and employees. Many organizations have realized the importance of diversity issues for they are inevitable necessities in our daily lives. Today, there are hundreds of organizations in the United States whose goals are to represent the most useful and comprehensive multicultural resources of AHANA (African, Hispanic/Latino, Asian/Pacific Islander and Native American).

Discrimination

In previous chapters we learned about race, ethnicity, and ethnocentrism. Other catalysts of the challenges of diversity include gender, age, religion, ideology, national origin and sexual orientation, amongst others. Through a high level of prejudice and biases some people discriminate against other people who possess different characteristics. Discrimination is a biased decision based on a prejudice against an individual or a group characterized by race, class, sexual orientation, age, disabilities, etc. It generally happens when the majority of any group confront representatives of minority groups. Examples of such include dominant white versus black, dominant males versus females, dominant young versus elderly people (or vice-versa), dominant rich versus the poor, and so forth.

In every multiracial society there are different ways of life that are generated from cultural differences. People are diverse because of their race, ethnicities, beliefs, ideologies, orientations, and preferences. The norm that has been identified by many people in multicultural America is the *ism* configurations that make the spectrum of challenges. Haessly (2001) asserts that much of the problems in our society stem from our "isms." These "isms" such as racism, sexism, ageism, ableism, classism, and many more are challenges of diversity and shall destroy every society:

> Each 'ism' impacts on both the personal and the public levels of our lives. At the personal level, the internalization of beliefs and attitudes affect how we view each other and relate to each other in our families, neighborhoods, workplaces, and the world. At the public level, these attitudes and beliefs are institutionalized in our government, education, and business policies, practices, and programs. When such policies and practices based on gender, skin color, cultural and religious differences, age or ability level, or some other criteria are institutionalized, it leads to exclusion; the uneven and unfair distribution of power and resources; and the establishment of laws and policies which favor one group over another (p. 148).

Racism

The world will never forget the Holocaust—a shameful product of racism by the Nazi regime of Hitler in Germany where more than 6 million Jews were murdered in concentration camps. No human beings can justify this atrocity in the history of mankind. Those who survived from the Holocaust since World War II have documented the crimes in many ways. The most remarkable collection of Holocaust crimes is on display at the Holocaust Museum in Washington D.C. This historical testimonial is an important place to visit for many tourists from all over the United States and around the world.

Many nations around the world teach their children historical facts that have taken place in the two world wars. The Holocaust is one of those sad subjects of history that will never be forgotten. In the United States, children learn about the Holocaust and Holocaust survivors in middle school. In 1998, a small town middle school in Tennessee made a historical event by collecting 6 million paper clips to help eighth grade students visualize the number of Jews killed in Nazi concentration camps (see full story at the end of the chapter).

People who deny the entire tragedy of the Holocaust are called Holocaust deniers. Among them are Nazi group, skinhead groups, and other close-minded people who believe that this atrocity never happened. Much to their consternation, historical evidence and testimonial documents are open to the public in museums and galleries around the world.

On May 17, 2004 Americans celebrated the 50th anniversary of Brown vs. Board of Education (discussed in chapter 6) all around the country. In comparison with fifty years ago, the United States has achieved a great victory over hatred, defamation, inequality, and classism. There were many press conferences, rallies, and gatherings to remember the legacy of those who gave their lives to struggle for freedom, social justice, and anti-discrimination. It was widely argued, in major metropolitan areas, that segregation has not been entirely decimated. The main theme of Brown vs. Board of Education focused on the issue of segregation which the media kept in the news. "Separate and unequal remain," argued Senator John Kerry, the presidential nominee on May 17, 2004. Community leaders expressed their opinions that justice and equality have not prevailed in some aspects of life. They argued that there's an obvious re-segregation in some urban areas.

Clyde W. Ford (1994, p. 11) in his work, *We Can all get Along: 50 Steps You Can Take to Help End Racism*, writes: "Racist behavior has declined, but racist attitudes have not." In recent years, the faces of discrimination in the context of racism and classism are portrayed in many areas of the country. In the winter of 2003, a white woman refused to sit next to a black woman in Orchestra Hall in downtown Minneapolis. "…Abercrombie and Fitch is back on the hot-seat – this time for racial discrimination in hiring practices," says Carrie Ching, a free-lance journalist and an editor for WireTap (Ching, 2003). She explains that Abercrombie hires white people only for sales floor jobs and keeps other ethnic groups such as black, Latino, and Asians in the stock room and away from the public in order to epitomize their company's motto the "classic American look." There could be many more companies whose unknown practices in racial discrimination would not be tolerated by the majority of Americans. Not long ago, Denny's Restaurant was under scrutiny for discriminating against people of color.

No one more than a colored person can describe the race-class scenario so well. Ching (2003), portrays that "When you go to an expensive restaurant, the managers and servers are almost always white, while the busboys and kitchen help are unfailingly people of color." She also describes a scenario that can be observed in many organizations these days. "Diversity is great, but only when it happens at the lower levels of an organization so as not to challenge the skewed balance of power. The signs are everywhere."

In Spring 2004, a colleague visited Gulf Port-Biloxi, two little pleasure towns adjacent to each other along the Gulf of Mexico in Mississippi and noticed that people still have issues with diversity. He stated that "People look at you noticeably because you are a colored person—black, brown, light brown, Asian, Middle Eastern, any but white." In some states this perception still exists. It is the way America was formed and this attitude will remain for quite some time. "Race still plays a major if unspoken role in the way our society is organized (Ching, 2003)."

Michael Eric Dyson (Dyson, 1996) the author of *Race Rules: Navigating the Color Line* argues that "Race and racism are not static forces. They mutate, grow, transform, and are redefined in complex ways. Understanding racial mystification helps us grasp the hidden premises, buried perceptions, and cloaked meanings of race as they show up throughout our culture." (p. 35)

A white student of mine, without any reservation, confessed that "It's hard not to be a racist!" He stressed that his father is a racist, his mother is a racist, and, so is he! He continued: "I grew up in a prejudiced family with no association with diversity. In my neighborhood there wasn't any person different from us. Hatred is a kind of family value. Obviously, my ancestors were bigots too! With this lifestyle do you expect me to be open-minded and tolerant?" Ella Mazel (1998) quoted psychologist and social scientist Kenneth B. Clark about invisible racism: "Students, research workers and professionals in the behavioral sciences—like members of the clergy and educators—are no more immune by virtue of their values and training to the diseases and superstitions of American racism than is the average man."

A challenge that I had in one of my classes changed to a positive experience. One of my students showed anger and a negative attitude on almost every subject we discussed. In the middle of the course, he could not resist any longer and made a rude comment that was not appropriate for the class. I asked him to leave, he refused. So, I had him removed from the class by the security person. He was suspended for a few sessions. He met with the dean, our department director, and his counselor. He promised the dean to behave himself for the remaining period of the course. I allowed him to come back to class. He came to me and apologized with tears in his eyes for what he did. At the end of the course he wrote an excellent final project, explaining how difficult it was not to be a racist living in a household where all were prejudiced. He admitted that the cultural diversity course changed his life. He wants to be open-minded and respect people from other cultures. At the end of the course he shook hands with me and thanked me for this positive experience.

While America has a long way to go in terms of racial equality, some organizations do care about racial discrimination and denigration vis-à-vis diverse personnel. An example was mentioned to me by a former student explaining that one of his former employers did something about racial issues in their workplace. One day a racial slur was discovered on the men's room door. The management held a company wide meeting to make the situation clear to everyone and to find the perpetrator. Since no one came forward to confess or cooperate with any information regarding the incident, the bathroom door was sent to a crime laboratory for handwriting analysis. The company was so adamant and demonstrated zero tolerance on this matter, yet no conclusion was ever made about the whole incident. Albeit, no one was accused of this prejudice, the company showed strong concern and took the diversity issue seriously.

In order to understand the challenges of diversity that are created via discrimination one should perceive and understand the concept of dominant privilege. Dominant privilege is the source of oppression, inequality and other notorious treatments that non-dominant groups are the victims of. (Heuberger, 2001)

Peggy McIntosh, the associate director of the Center for Research on Women at Wellesley College in Massachusetts is frequently quoted about "White Privilege." She writes that as a white person, she realized that she had been taught about racism as something that places other people at a disadvantage, and had been taught to exclude the consequential aspects of white privilege which places her at an advantage. She also asserts that the majority of white students in the United States think that racism does not affect them due to the fact that they are not people of color; in other words, they do not see their "whiteness" as a racial identity (Mazel, 1998).

Classism

In order to identify classism, one should know the meaning of "class" first. Class and socio-economic status are interchangeable. In other words, class refers to relative social rank in terms of income, wealth, status, and/or power. Classism, therefore, refers to a set of practices and beliefs that could be institutional, cultural, or individual while allocating differential value to people based on their socio-economic values. As a result, excessive inequality prevails causing unmet basic human needs (Adams, et al, 1997).

There is no doubt that the challenges of diversity create hatred, animosity, and therefore turmoil in any society. They are disruptive to any human environment and should be considered as a stumbling block for success and productivity in the workplace.

Racism and classism do exist everywhere in the world. One of the most well-known examples of classism is the caste system in India. Through the eyes of the ruling class and the minds of the dominant privileged those who have no power, no wealth, and are homeless or live in shanty quarters are called "untouchables." These under privileged and destitute human beings who represent a large group in India are not allowed to enter the elite's territories. If they did, they would be belligerently insulted and kicked out by the members of the elite group.

Sexism

Male against female mentality and vice-versa exists in many societies. The magnitude of this problem varies from culture to culture.

In the United States, where democracy and human rights are more protected and appreciated, people try to eliminate factors that contribute to prejudice or bias regarding the sexes. The male chauvinistic attitude towards the opposite sex is an example of sexism. The pattern of sexism is quite revealing when you visit those societies where women's rights are violated.

Generally speaking, sexism is the presenting of more attributes and orientations towards one sex. For example, in recent years sexism has been the controversial issue in advertising. Some marketing specialists portray their products leaning towards men or women for having a successful sale. "Sex appeal and sexual stereotype are still used to sell many products." (Kornblum & Julian, 2004)

Speaking of sexes and sexism, it is appropriate to know about feminism and eliminate some confusion about this movement. Feminism is a controversial issue in the United States. Its definition varies from source to source. According to amazoncastle.com (2004), "Feminism is a theory that men and women should be equal politically, economically and socially." Sometimes this definition is also referred to as "core feminism" or "core feminist theory." Notice that this theory does not subscribe to differences between men and women *or* similarities between men and women, nor does it refer to excluding men or only furthering women's causes. Most other branches of feminism do. *Why* you believe in feminism and *what* your ideas are to make feminism a reality is what causes arguments within the feminism movement.

Ageism

This challenge is not centralized for elderly people only. It is a subject of discrimination for young people as well. The same way that we may think about an old person when it comes to the ability to do a job regardless of experience, also becomes an issue of consideration for a young person when it comes to lack of experience to do a job regardless of ability. No matter if an individual is old or young, age discrimination may happen anywhere. Although age has been the subject of discrimination in the workplace for decades, it should be noted however, that ageism is geared more often towards elderly people than the younger generation. Cultural norms demonstrate how an individual deals with an aged person. Many cultures have special respect for their elders. And the way to show it is to take care of their elders themselves rather than sending them to nursing homes.

An example of ageism was recently portrayed in the made for CBS television movie "Remembering of the Middle-aged Woman" which starred Christine Lahti as a newspaper editor who was fired so that a much younger, prettier woman could have her job. When the younger woman failed at her job, the boss called the older woman to offer her old job back. Her response: "I don't need to work for a sexist, ageist, scum-sucking pig."

Experts have demonstrated many patterns of association with ageism in different countries. Again, this may vary from culture to culture as people proceed with how to handle the problem. In many western societies, young generations have less tolerance for elderly people when they interact with them. A bank teller may have less patience for an older customer. A clerk in a grocery store may dislike waiting on an elderly customer. There are numerous examples of how young people disassociate themselves with the elderly.

Aging and Generation

Aging or geriatric studies have been a subject of sociology for many decades. Living conditions and appearing in public for the aging is different from culture to culture. An eighty year old person may still be capable or willing to drive in the United States, while the same age person in another country may sit at home all day long. Apparently, the former may create some hard feeling for younger people who think an 80 year old should not be allowed to drive and slow the traffic. The latter, on the other hand may receive more attention and respect and feel revered and recognized as a wise person among many younger members of the family, relatives, and neighbors.

This social matter is becoming more alarming as baby boomers soon will be an unprecedented huge number of elderly people in the United States. The baby boom refers to a large increase in the birthrate, especially in the U.S. from 1946 through 1964. There is no doubt that 72 million baby boomers will soon impact the age and aging in this country.

The aging issue brings about the subject of the "generation gap," a term coined by Margaret Mead (1901-1978), a noted American anthropologist and writer in 1960s. Each generation has its own identity, beliefs, values, way of life, and honors. For example *The*

Greatest Generation by Tom Brokaw, is a tribute to the members of the World War II generation. We also have generation X and generation Y. According to Kottak & Kozaitis (2003) Generation X refers to 17 million Americans born between 1961 and 1975 and Generation Y or "Millennium generation" recognizes 60 million Americans born between 1976 and 1999. My father, myself, and my son are from three different generations with values, beliefs, and mindsets that collectively separate us ideologically. This chasm that is now evident universally was the talk of the nation back in 1960s when young generations unlike their elders opposed the idea of the U.S. engagement in the Vietnam War. Today, history is repeating itself— we are witnessing the same confrontation as the generation gap—that is, the War in Afghanistan and Iraq, and other social issues imposed upon us in recent years.

Ableism

Some people with ability have no patience or tolerance for other people with disability. The feeling and attitude about ability versus disability is called ableism. Generally, it is related to discrimination against disabled people that is committed from people with ability. It is very important to know about disability in general and disability status in particular in cultural diversity.

The rights of disabled people gained attention a few decades ago, or to be exact, during the historical period of the civil rights movement. In 1990, the Americans with Disabilities Act (ADA) was signed into law. This Act protects disabled peoples' rights in employment, in public transportation, and in other public facilities that are duly available to other individuals who are not mentally or physically challenged.

It is estimated that more than 6 million people in the United States have a permanent physical or mental disability (Heuberger, 2001).

There is an ongoing debate about *handicapped* and *disabled*. For example, those who are physically challenged do not like to be called handicapped. Technically, there is a difference between handicapped and disabled. According to Health and Human Services (HHS), handicapped are those individuals who are disfigured, retarded, mentally ill, emotionally disabled, or drug or alcohol addicted, as well as those with histories of cancer and heart disease (Kornblum & Julian, 2004).

On the other hand, disabilities are limitations that interrupt everyday activities such as self-care, mobility, communication, interactions with relatives and friends, as well as employment. Disabled people in the United States have the advantage of receiving assistance and training. They are provided with devices such as wheelchairs and hearing aids.

The status of disabilities changes to handicaps when everyday functions become impossible. If the environment is not equipped with devices to accommodate disabled persons, then the condition of disability is considered a handicap. In other words, physical barriers are the cause of handicaps (Welch Schrank, 1995).

Equal Rights vs. Inequality

In many societies around the world the basic rights of people are violated. The ruling minority or the dominant power never allows citizens to have their voices heard, or otherwise they would be persecuted. In the United States of America where democracy is the keystone of national politics, freedom and equal rights are at the forefront of the governing body. Some experts believe that only 40-45% of the countries in the world practicing democracy. In America, equal rights are more the matter of discussion than in any other part of the world, yet individuals are mystified by the deficiency still of "equal rights" when it comes to education, employment, job promotion, housing, mortgage loans, same sex marriage, and matters as such.

Melba Pattillo Beals, one of the Little Rock Arkansas Nine and a civil rights activist writes: "Does anybody really think we wanted to go to Central High School because we wanted to sit next to white people? We wanted to go to Central High School because they were getting Rhodes Scholarships there. We wanted equal access to opportunities" (Mazel, 1998, p. 49).

Employment Disarray

For many years employment was in chaos in the United States. After the period of the depression in America, the predominantly white population had less difficulty finding a job than people of color. The main obstacle was obviously prejudice stemming from racism. "In 1963, finding a decent job was still very difficult for blacks in America. Black unemployment stood at 11%, while for whites the figure was just 5%. And whereas a white family earned, on average, about $6,500 a year, a black family earned $3,500 a year" (Williams, 2001, p. 197).

Perhaps 10 years after the civil rights movement, in the early 1970s, the cloud of discrimination over employment gradually moved away but never disappeared entirely although Title VII of the Civil Rights Act of 1964 prohibits discrimination in many aspects of the employment relationship (Law Information Institute, 2003). Many forms of discrimination such as bias in hiring, promotion, job assignments, termination, compensation, pregnancy, religion, national origin, sexual orientation, age, disability, as well as various kinds of harassments demonstrate employment disarray in the workplace. Another product of the laws of employment such as the Equal Employment Opportunity (EEO) leveled the uneven path of employment in the U.S. The Equal Employment Opportunity Commission (EEOC) oversees employment discrimination in U.S. work environments. Today, many employers carry the slogan of "Equal Opportunity Employer" (EOE), yet some violate the law by not recognizing that they may get caught by the EEOC for discriminating against white people too.

Employment discrimination has impacted many minorities other than just African Americans and women, such as foreign born individuals (immigrants) and homosexual citizens. Even legal protections for gays and lesbians in this country are significantly more limited compared to other diverse groups. A homosexual man I know, being downsized by his previous employer, was unemployed for two years before he was able to get a clerical job with a mortgage company. According to the National Opinion Research Center (NORC), we are now more tolerant of open discussions regarding homosexuality than we were 10 or 20 years ago. Surveys reveal that almost 50% of Americans have difficulty accepting homosexuality, therefore they think homosexuals should be prohibited from certain jobs that they are qualified for, vis-à-vis working with young people (Kornblum & Julian, 2004).

It is sad to say that discrimination on the basis of national origin has always been, and unfortunately remains to be, a damaging force in American society (Massaro, 1996). A foreign born educator had an extremely difficult time to get a job either with the government or with private companies. After five years of constant struggles and accumulating more than 200 rejection letters he finally found a job with an academic institution.

The words of Clarence Page (Mazel, 1998, p. 115) suggest that "equal opportunity" should be provided at early stages of life when kids are shaping up their personalities:

> America will not have racial equality until opportunities are equalized, beginning at the preschool level, to build up the supply of qualified applicants for the new jobs emerging in information-age America. The American ideal of equal opportunity still produces rewards, when it is given a real try. It needs to be tried more often.

Harassment

Today, the issue of harassment in the workplace has become a matter of controversy. Basically, human resources departments of each organization oversee issues such as sexual harassment, equal employment opportunity, affirmative action, and any kind of discrimination that violates individual rights. In cultural diversity, the issue of harassment is discussed when individuals are harassed based on their differences and uniqueness such as religion, sexual orientation, gender, political affiliation, general appearance, size, weight, age, or other matters that the dominant workforce does not possess or has a hard time accepting. Frequently, individuals who choose a special life style such as a punk, a Goth, or a grunge find it disturbing in workplaces where diversity has not been accepted as uniqueness and a human quality.

With a widely recognized importance of diversity in organizations around the country, special emphasis has been given to discriminatory attitudes in the workplace that are stumbling blocks to the success and progress of any work environment. People with different beliefs and ritual practices find it uncomfortable to demonstrate their daily routines. The understanding of different cultures and ethnicities provide opportunities for all to understand the sensitivity of their coworkers who are coming from different backgrounds. For example, Muslims pray five times a day, of which at least one time occurs around noon and requires the worshiper to do it in the workplace. Women of Muslim faith—those who are extremists should wear a *hijab*, namely to cover their head and body at all times when out in the public. In the month of Ramadan, these Muslim worshipers observe fasting which deprives them from eating, drinking, and smoking from dawn to dusk. Orthodox Jews wear *yarmulke* on their heads, eat kosher items, and must not work during the *Sabetha* starting from Friday evening to Saturday evening. Indian Sikhs wear turbans and may wear traditional outfits to work. Africans may choose to wear their traditional clothes such as *Dashiki* or *Babariga*. The list goes on and on as we explore different cultures. The above are just a few examples describing different life styles and preferences which appear in our multicultural nation and from time to time the main stream culture may not tolerate them due to a lack of awareness and understanding.

Affirmative Action

The subject of affirmative action has been very controversial and caused heated debate over the last two decades or so. It is important to mention this in the cultural diversity realm due to the fact that it impacts the lives of many individuals who are from different backgrounds, especially people of color. Generally speaking, affirmative action is a policy or program that seeks to redress past discrimination by increasing opportunities for underrepresented groups as in education or employment. Andrew Young, a civil rights activist and the U.S. Ambassador to the United Nations in Jimmy Carter's presidency, expresses that "Fairness as well as logic requires that special consideration be given to people who have been locked out of the economic mainstream" (Mazel, 1998, p. 118). In other words, affirmative action was designed to ensure entry into schools and job markets that had been unavailable to women, minorities, all people of color (Harper & Appel, 2001).

According to Edwin C. Hettinger, professor and author, affirmative action is also called reverse discrimination by some people. He argues that in a general sense "affirmative action" or "reverse discrimination" is hiring or admitting a somehow less well qualified female or black male in lieu of rather somehow more qualified white male to compensate injustices women and black males have undergone or to even eliminate sexual and/or racial inequality they have experienced in the past and even in the present time (Larmer, 1996). This, basically, is what the general public thinks of affirmative action. Also, as they have been informed by the media, people think of a kind of weaker affirmative action which Hettinger refers to as "…giving preference to minority candidates only when qualifications are equal, or providing special educational opportunities for youths in disadvantaged groups." (Larmer, 1996, p. 432). Colin Powell, the state secretary (2000-2004), said in 1995, that "…affirmative action in the best sense promotes equal consideration, not reverse discrimination." (Mazel, 1998, p. 118) In other words, if women, African Americans, Hispanics, Asians, and other diverse people in the United States were employed the same way predominant Whites were recruited there would be no need for affirmative action to be created.

On June 22, 2003, affirmative action reached its highest controversial level in U.S. history. On this day, the Supreme Court ruled affirmative action to be law. The case of the University of Michigan reached the Supreme Court and in conclusion five U.S. Supreme Court justices voted for affirmative action. Now that affirmative action is signed into law it should be respected by American citizens regardless of personal negative feelings.

Arthur Fletcher is hailed as "the father of affirmative action." Fletcher advised four presidents: Nixon, Ford, Reagan and George H.W. Bush. He also served as a delegate to the United Nations, and as an executive director of the United Negro College Fund. He died in July 2005 at the age of 80 (DiversityInc.com, 2005).

Benefits of Diversity

In many parts of the world diversity may not mean very much, or may even be hard to translate in a particular language, because it may not seem very important at all. As we mentioned before, in America, Canada, Australia, and some European countries, where ethnic groups chose to settle and make a new life, diversity means a lot. Yet, in the United States, when we talk about diversity some think it refers only to "blacks," some define it as "affirmative action" or some may think about "minorities." The fact of the matter is that diversity is all of that, and much more. Once more, it is important to say that diversity is synonymous with a variety that includes not only differences but similarities as well. As we ponder the world of diversity, organizations should value and acknowledge all areas of diversity including but not limited to race/ethnicity, gender, sexual orientation, disability, learning styles, age, and religion. Diversity does not only represent challenges in society and in particular in the workplace, it provides benefits that the majority does not realize until they directly benefit from it.

Uniqueness and Innovation

When we talk about diversity in an organization, mainly the focus is on the variety of human resources that shape the organization. It is extremely important to explore the talents and uniqueness of individuals which may have been hidden for a long time. Not many people are comfortable with presenting themselves. It is up to the leadership team to recognize their unique resources and value them continuously. People who come from different backgrounds, bring a variety of values with them. Paramahansa Yogananda (1893-1952), an Indian spiritual teacher and a pioneer of Yoga in the West, once said that we are destined to learn from different cultures, so that we may select their best qualities and harmonize them with our own behavior. For example, in a working environment where there are people from a variety of places in the world, a collection of ideas and innovations are at hand. Obviously, people who react with enthusiasm and put passion into their work, are considered the company's assets. The innovations and advances that diverse groups share with their American co-workers can be remarkable.

Diversity goes beyond gender and race. It travels all around the world, due to the fact that large corporations, these days, establish units around the world or plan global expansion (Thomas, 1996). In chapter 10 we will learn more about globalization and the expansion of corporate America.

Resourcefulness and Creativity

Working together, building up teamwork, and organizing useful planning are the tools of success in any organization, no matter how small the organization. A neighborhood activity on fundraising, a challenge of environmental protection or unity on disease prevention all require effort, employing ideas, and the effective mobilization of available resources. In this respect, people from different cultures and backgrounds provide the framework we need to achieve our goals.

Throughout history we learned how to deal with people from other regions who were initially strangers. Either exploration brought them to us, or perhaps the intent of invasion and exploitation was the primary cause. At any rate, we communed with invaders and intruders and life continued its normal course.

Consider you are working in a company with a predominantly Anglo-Saxon culture featuring the same set routine for production and development. Now, imagine you are part of a working environment where there are more than 40 ethnic groups represented and at least more than six members of the leadership team are representing different cultures. Obviously the former build-up is not as resourceful or creative as the latter one. When people from different backgrounds bring ideas and innovations to the table, the result of the end-product is amazing.

For example, in marketing and advertising companies in the United States, teams on styles and fashions include creative individuals from different countries. These expatriates, come to the United States for further education, stay here after graduation, find suitable jobs, decide to reside in the land of opportunity, and prefer not to return to their countries. These unique men and women possess a plethora of experiences in their respective professions which produce outstanding results embedded in innovative imaginations.

When employees are from different backgrounds, the impact of their deep differences on certain areas provide a remarkable success for the company. Juanita Nanez, Vice President of Diversity at Carlson Restaurants Worldwide, in a personal interview, says it all:

> "At Carlson Restaurants Worldwide we recognize that people and their individuality are our most dynamic resource. We value the individual differences - the different backgrounds, experiences, perspectives and ideas of everyone. We believe that those differences make our company stronger by allowing us to make better decisions and being able to better respond to the needs of all of our guests, employees, business partners and communities."

In the context of diversity's benefits, we should look into the avenues and opportunities suggested by Sonnenschein (1997, pp. 3-4):

Diversity:

- Enables a wide range of views to be present in an organization, including views that might challenge the status quo from all sides.
- Focuses and strengthens an organization's core values.
- Is instrumental in organizational change.
- Stimulates social, economic, intellectual, and emotional growth.
- Helps an organization understand its place in the global community

Many organizations have embraced diversity in a number of ways, to foster their future directions. Avon, a 112 year-old partner in the American marketplace has achieved the pinnacle of celebrating diversity after a long experience with diversity issues. Avon's commitment to a diverse workforce and setting an effective plan to mange diversity for the organization is a good pattern for many organizations to follow. (Thomas, 1996)

Interconnectedness and cooperation

In today's world or for a better clarification, in the 21st century, we need to get acquainted with "paradigms"—a pattern or a model that allows us to explain or investigate phenomena as we wish to explore or study for a better understanding. A paradigm is a transporter that takes us to many positive places. The paradigm of cooperation brings positive energy to do things with good feelings. Once we acknowledge our differences and work around them, the arena for connection and cooperation becomes more available. In this friendly atmosphere, similarities supersede differences and individuals interconnect using positive attitudes to generate a relationship they never thought it would be possible to achieve.

The most prevalent example of cooperation can be found in the workplace. Quality working relationships are the essence of productivity and progressive outcomes. Diversity in organizations is the conduit for success if interconnectedness and cooperation are recognized as central parts of the operation. Teamwork and valuing group prosperity have revitalized the American individualistic culture. Williams (2001), emphasizes working together and building a sense of community by saying that "we must create a way to structure our collective efforts so that everyone prospers." With this attitude we should be able to enter the gate of solidarity in order to work, live, and thrive in the land of diversity.

Synergy

What is this "synergy" that some corporate presenters talk about these days? How does it relate to diversity? If you have not looked into the meaning of this unique word, now is the time to find out the benefit we may get from creating synergy in our organizational system. P.E. Randeria, an organization and management development consultant, has a lot to say about synergy. She defines synergy as "...a combined, cooperative action of independent or separate parts that result in a greater whole. ...synergy implies the inherent necessity of combining variety and differences for growth, creativity, and change" (Randeria, 2001, p. 130).

It is apparent that synergy is the keystone of collaboration in a multi-talented workplace which brings a variety of creativity and virtual change for success and development. But, the first step is a positive relationship. In corporate America, where employees represent a variety of national origins, and as a result a variety of differences, relationship plays an important part of participation towards common goals. According to Lewis Brown Griggs, the co-author of *Valuing Diversity: New Tools for a New Reality*, "Relationship facilitates increased participation and thereby greater opportunity for synergy (3 x 4 instead of 3 + 4)" (Griggs & Louw, 1995, p. 210).

Synergy plays a substantial role in diversity. We may benefit from synergy in many ways in our community, in our work environment, and in any form of public organization. Randeria (2001) shows us how to create synergy in the midst of diversity:

-**Step One**: To create a shared understanding of the existing issues and concerns of the work group in relation to the task at hand.

-**Step Two**: To create a process in which people feel free to communicate. In a free environment people are assured that they will be heard, understood, and recognized. In this respect, they can share their experiences and perspectives with no reservations.

-**Step Three**: To teach the essential competencies by utilizing the following:

- To know how to establish boundaries, rules, and context in any situation and interaction
- To have personal awareness, accessibility, and understanding of these boundaries
- To understand personal values based upon experiences and background
- To be able and ready to explore, discuss, and work interdependently

Having had all these steps employed into a framework, synergy begins to generate a powerful environment where spiritual, psychological, and personal achievements are the tools of success for a positive and energetic relationship.

The Paper Clip Project

Source: NBC's The Jane Pauley Show, December 30, 2004.

Recently, the Whitwell Middle School in Tennessee conducted a project to honor Holocaust victims and sympathize with the Holocaust survivors. In social studies class the eight graders could not vision the magnitude of 6 million human beings killed in the Holocaust by the Nazis. The social studies teacher, the vice principal and the principal came with the idea of collecting paper clips to show students how big 6 million can be. By writing letters to many famous people in the nation and around the world they asked for one received paper clip donations. Initially, paper clip image was originated from Norway at the time of Holocaust to signify the atrocity of innocent people killed in the Nazi concentration camps. The response was incredible. Almost 30 million paper clips were sent by open-minded people to this small town middle school in Tennessee. A German journalist couple were excited about this project became connected with the organizers and the students involved in the project. The problem was then where to store all these paper clips. The school principal Linda Hooper came with the idea that it would be appropriate if they could place all these paper clips in a real railcar used during the Holocaust. With the efforts of the German journalists, a railcar was located in a museum in Germany, was purchased and arranged to be brought to the United States. Today, the Whitwell Middle School is the sight of this historic Holocaust railcar where all of the collected paper clips are stored in honor of the Holocaust victims who were killed by the Nazi in World War II. Miramax has made an excellent documentary on this project which is a must-see. This is another historic event that can not be denied by Holocaust deniers.

Summary

Diversity is a complex phenomenon with a variety of features. Diversity presents challenges and benefits. Diversity challenges are discrimination such as racism and classism. Other "isms" such as sexism, ageism, ableism, and ethnocentrism, to name a few, are also regarded as challenges of diversity. These invitations to discrimination create obstacles for employment. Equal opportunity and affirmative action have been in the center of diversity in recent decades, mainly because of race and gender, and personal orientations towards certain aspects of life in a democratic society such as in the United States.

Diversity does not revolve around challenges only. It has benefits too. To some people, unfortunately, the benefits of diversity are not so obvious. The most recognized benefits of diversity are creativity, innovation, cooperation, and synergy. These characteristics evolve in environments where people from different cultural backgrounds work or live together; in industries, in educational facilities, in the market place and in local communities. The benefits of diversity should be praised while challenges are to be minimized for a peaceful multicultural society.

Test Your Knowledge

Part One: Select the best choice.

Instruction: In front of each statement below put "A" for agree, "D" for disagree, and "N" for neutral.

1.____ The tap root of racism is almost 400 years long.

2.____History reveals that the English created the notion of 'black laborers' which led to slavery in America.

3.____"Separate and unequal remain" despite Brown vs. Board of Education success.

4.____"No one more than a person of color can describe the race-class scenario so well."

5.____"Dominant privilege is the source of oppression, inequality and other notorious treatments that non-dominant groups are the victims of."

6.____ The paradigm of cooperation brings positive energy to do things with good feelings.

7.____ Diversity does not revolve around challenges only.

8.____Affirmative action is reverse discrimination.

9.____Diversity stimulates social, economic, intellectual, and emotional growth.

10.____Discrimination is not always against people of color, Caucasians may be the subject of discrimination too.

11.____ Disabled people in the United States have the advantage of receiving assistance and training.

12.____ Synergy implies the inherent necessity of combining variety and differences for growth, creativity, and change.

Part Two: Discussion Questions

1. Why is racism associated with slavery?
2. Explain why race and racism are not static forces?
3. What are the causes of discrimination?
4. Why should we teach our children about the Holocaust?
5. What do Holocaust survivors contribute to diversity?
6. Is feminism a kind of sexism?
7. Why should gay and lesbian rights be protected?
8. How can you create synergy in your workplace?
9. What is the difference between "handicapped" and "disabled"?

10. How does the concept of the baby boom affect the problem of age and aging in the U.S.?

11. How does affirmative action impact diversity?

12. According to Peggy McIntosh's argument "white students in the United States think that racism does not affect them." What is your reaction to her argument?

13. Explain why the challenges of diversity disrupt the workplace.

MEDIUM PROUD   By Lee B. Erickson

I am medium proud
Slightly raw and riding
mid way through
the parade of life,
not leading the charge
nor watching
from the sidelines.

I am medium proud.
When asked I smile and
clearly state I'm gay
no longer hiding behind
the labels, tags or
stereotypes used by others
to define me.

I am medium proud.
Walking with my
head held high,
choosing to be
hated for who I am than
loved for all that others
wish I would be
but know in their hearts
I am not.

Still hoping and
dreaming
of being loved for
who I am.

I am medium proud
Not rare or well-done.
Medium.
Misunderstood,
I am medium proud.
Medium proud.
Medium proud.

Chapter 6: The Quest for Recognition

"We will reach the goal of freedom in Birmingham and all over the nation, because the goal of America is freedom. Abused and scorned though we may be, our destiny is tied up with America's destiny."

-Dr. Martin Luther King, Jr.

Objectives

- Identify the challenge of Black America for peace and freedom
- Recognize the major events of the American Civil Rights Movement
- Explore the historical significance of the civil rights movement
- Evaluate the impact of unrest and turmoil on the well-being of the public
- Comprehend the chaotic atmosphere of 1950-1960
- Assess the post-civil rights movement in America
- Appreciate the legacy of Dr. Martin Luther King, Jr.
- Distinguish the philosophy of civil rights leaders

The Civil Rights Movement

On July 2, 2004 Americans remembered the 40th anniversary of one of the most remarkable events in American history—the Civil Rights Act that was signed into law on July 2, 1964.

Julian Bond, the NAACP chairman of the board, argues that the civil rights movement started as early as the seventeenth century. In the 1940s, when he was a teenager, he remembers the beginning of the uprising against injustice and the lack of freedom. He asserts that "…for most Americans, the civil rights movement began on May 17, 1954, when the Supreme Court handed down the Brown v. Board of

Education of Topeka decision outlawing segregation in public schools" (Williams, 2001, p. XI).

Julian Bond's explanation about the Civil Rights movement (from the introduction of *Eyes on the Prize*) is interesting:

> The civil rights movement in America began a long time ago. As early as the seventeenth century, blacks and whites, slaves in Virginia and Quakers in Pennsylvania, protested the barbarity of slavery. Nat Turner, Sojourner Truth, Fredrick Douglass, William Lloyd Garrison, John Brown, and Harriet Tubman are but a few of those who led the resistance to slavery before the Civil War. After the Civil War, another protracted battle began against slavery's legacy — racism and segregation. …The court unlocked the door, but the pressure applied by thousands of men and women in the movement pushed that door open wide enough to allow blacks to walk through it toward this country's essential prize: freedom (Williams, 2001, p. XI).

When you are not recognized for any reason in a gathering you feel demoralized and humiliated. Imagine what blacks and other minority groups went through for many years. That led to unrest and turmoil during the 1950s-1960s—the American Civil Rights movement.

Dr. Martin Luther King led the Civil Rights Movement and accomplished what he was dreaming of. He confessed that he had reached the mountaintop. He lived a short life but with dignity and glory, and many generations to come will learn from his legacy. In 21st century America we need to find out how much of MLK's dream has been accomplished and what else we need to do to carry on where he left off.

The Timeline of the American Civil Rights Movement

The following annotated events are the highlights of the Civil Rights Movement.

Plessy v. Ferguson

In 1890, the state of Louisiana passed a statue that all railway companies carrying passengers in their coaches should provide equal but separate accommodations for white and people of color. In 1892, Homer Plessy, a 30-year old black shoemaker, was jailed for sitting in the "white's" car of the East Louisiana Railroad. Plessy appeared in court and quarreled that the Separate Car Act violated the 13th and 14th Amendments of the Constitution. John Howard Ferguson, the judge, found Plessy guilty of refusing to leave the white car. After the Louisiana Supreme Court ruled in favor of Ferguson too, Plessy took the case to the U.S. Supreme Court but was found guilty again. The "separate but equal" precedent was set in the 1896 Plessy v. Ferguson ruling (Hartin, 1997).

Brown v. Board of Education

Oliver Brown, father of a third grader named Linda from Topeka, Kansas, was frustrated that his daughter had to travel a long way to a "black" school while there was a "white" elementary school in their neighborhood. Mr. Brown with the help of the NAACP, challenged this restriction up to the Supreme Court (Chafe, 2003). After three years of confrontation, in 1954 the Supreme Court finally ruled that the segregation of citizens is inherently unconstitutional. Justice Harlan's historic words greatly contributed to the ruling: "Our Constitution is color-blind, and neither knows nor tolerates classes among citizens. In respect of civil rights, all citizens are equal before the law..." The case of Brown v. Board of Education success ended the "separate but equal" law of the land (Hartin, 1997).

For more detailed information, refer to: *A History of Our Time*, by Chafe, et al (2003, pp. 193-198).

The Rosa Parks Incident

On December 1, 1955, in Montgomery, Alabama, a 42-year-old department store worker named Rosa Parks was arrested because she refused to give up her seat in the black section of the bus to a white man. The first four front rows of any bus were designated by the city to be reserved for white people. This incident led to explosive unrest that engaged community leaders, among them, Dr. Martin Luther King, Jr., in organizing a bus boycott. Martin Luther King, Jr., was arrested for the first time in his life due to the fact that Alabama law denied people the right to boycott. Coretta Scott King (Dr. King's wife) celebrated her husband's arrest for it would create national attention for the cause (William, 2001).

Blacks, who represented almost half of the city [Montgomery] population, did not ride a bus for [381 days]. Although it was extremely difficult for them to get to work, they suffered for the sake of their children and their grandchildren (Takaki, 1996). During this time, police brutality escalated, KKK terrors increased throughout the city, and the city officials including judges and the entire court system were behind the prejudice and bigotry against blacks. The Rosa Parks' episode and the bus boycott resulted in the Supreme Court decision that bus segregation was illegal.

Central High School, Little Rock, Arkansas

In 1957, President Eisenhower ordered 11,000 troops to Little Rock, Arkansas to control the situation escalated by an angry mob of 1,000 people and the Arkansas National Guardsmen who were ordered by the governor to prevent black students from entering the newly desegregated Little Rock High School (Heuberger, 2001). As a result, nine black teenagers (six females and three males) integrated Central High School. These courageous young individuals made a very difficult decision while angry mobs surfaced their violence over the controversial "integration."

For many years, segregation in the school systems around the country was a terrible nightmare for the black community amidst all the odds they were already struggling with. Dark days of suppression and hatred did not stop the decisiveness of those heroes and heroines, black and white, who put their lives in danger for a good cause. Thirty years after the Central High integration, all nine students had an opportunity to walk together and climb the steps of the school to be honored by Arkansas Governor Bill Clinton.

Melba Pattillo Beals, the writer of *Warriors Don't Cry* was one of the nine students who went through the ordeal of desegregation and chose to stand for her beliefs and dignity. She kept a journal of all of the events while in high school and used them to write her dramatic true story describing the inequality, hatred, tears, disappointments, and finally the sense of equality. Melba wrote: "I was only fifteen, and I was afraid for my life. But our dreams were stronger than their hatred." This young girl turned sixteen in 1957—the year she became a warrior on the front lines of the civil rights firestorm (Pattillo Beals, 1996).

Woolworth's, Greensboro, North Carolina, Incident

On February 2, 1960, at the Greensboro Woolworth's lunch counter three young black males named Joseph McNeil, Franklin McCain, and Billy Smith sat for lunch but were refused service. This resulted in a protest that inspired similar protests nationwide by many other blacks.

The Freedom Riders

In 1961, a year after the Greensboro Woolworth's lunch counter protest, the perpetrators of the acts of civil disobedience to integrate the interstate buses and bus terminals of the south became famous as "freedom riders." This defiant and brave coalition was guided by the Congress of Racial Equality (CORE), who encouraged black and white civil rights supporters to ride together in buses. Brutality showed its ugly face one more time when the "Freedom Riders" were beaten very badly by racist white mobs before T.V. cameras (Takaki, 1993).

The University of Mississippi Incident

The level of acceptance among white communities was very low despite the Supreme Court ruling which ended segregation in 1954. On September 30, 1962, as James Meredith (a black student) prepared to attend his first class the riot erupted on the University of Mississippi's campus. The mob included some three thousand individuals, students, local citizens, and Klan groups from Florida to Texas. They fought against U.S. Marshals with bricks, sticks, bottles, and homemade bombs. Despite the effort President Kennedy made to avoid it and by sending more than twenty thousand U.S. Army soldiers to restore order on the campus two students were killed and sixty marshals were wounded (usm.edu, 2000).

The 1963 Protest and "March on Washington"

Dr. Martin Luther King, Jr. and two other leaders, Reverend Abernathy and Reverend Shuttlesworth conducted nonviolent protests against segregation. They were all arrested and jailed. While in jail, Dr. King wrote the famous "Letter from the Birmingham Jail." On August 28, 1963, about 250,000 civil rights supporters gathered in Washington, in front of Lincoln Memorial. The "March on Washington" is famous for Dr. Martin Luther King's historic speech "I Have a Dream."

"I Have A Dream"
By Martin Luther King, Jr.

Delivered on the steps at the Lincoln Memorial in Washington D.C. on August 28, 1963.

Source: Martin Luther King, Jr.: The Peaceful Warrior, Pocket Books, NY, 1968.

Five score years ago, a great American, in whose symbolic shadow we stand signed the Emancipation Proclamation. This momentous decree came as a great beacon light of hope to millions of Negro slaves who had been seared in the flames of withering injustice. It came as a joyous daybreak to end the long night of captivity. But one hundred years later, we must face the tragic fact that the Negro is still not free.

One hundred years later, the life of the Negro is still sadly crippled by the manacles of segregation and the chains of discrimination. One hundred years later, the Negro lives on a lonely island of poverty in the midst of a vast ocean of material prosperity. One hundred years later, the Negro is still languishing in the corners of American society and finds himself an exile in his own land.

So we have come here today to dramatize an appalling condition. In a sense we have come to our nation's capital to cash a check. When the architects of our republic wrote the magnificent words of the Constitution and the Declaration of Independence, they were signing a promissory note to which every American was to fall heir.

This note was a promise that all men would be guaranteed the inalienable rights of life, liberty, and the pursuit of happiness. It is obvious today that America has defaulted on this promissory note insofar as her citizens of color are concerned. Instead of honoring this sacred obligation, America has given the Negro people a bad check which has come back marked "insufficient funds." But we refuse to believe that the bank of justice is bankrupt. We refuse to believe that there are insufficient funds in the great vaults of opportunity of this nation.

So we have come to cash this check -- a check that will give us upon demand the riches of freedom and the security of justice. We have also come to this hallowed spot to remind America of the fierce urgency of now. This is no time to engage in the luxury of cooling off or to take the tranquilizing drug of gradualism. Now is the time to rise from the dark and desolate valley of segregation to the sunlit path of racial justice. Now is the time to open the doors of opportunity to all of God's children. Now is the time to lift our nation from the quicksands of racial injustice to the solid rock of brotherhood.

It would be fatal for the nation to overlook the urgency of the moment and to underestimate the determination of the Negro. This sweltering summer of the Negro's legitimate discontent will not pass until there is an invigorating autumn of freedom and equality. Nineteen sixty-three is not an end, but a beginning. Those who hope that the Negro needed to blow off steam and will now be content will have a rude awakening if the nation returns to business as usual. There will be neither rest nor tranquility in America until the Negro is granted his citizenship rights.

The whirlwinds of revolt will continue to shake the foundations of our nation until the bright day of justice emerges. But there is something that I must say to my people who stand on the warm threshold which leads into the palace of justice. In the process of gaining our rightful place we must not be guilty of wrongful deeds. Let us not seek to satisfy our thirst for freedom by drinking from the cup of bitterness and hatred.

We must forever conduct our struggle on the high plane of dignity and discipline. we must not allow our creative protest to degenerate into physical violence. Again and again we must rise to the majestic heights of meeting physical force with soul force.

The marvelous new militancy which has engulfed the Negro community must not lead us to distrust of all white people, for many of our white brothers, as evidenced by their presence here today, have come to realize that their destiny is tied up with our destiny and their freedom is inextricably bound to our freedom.

We cannot walk alone. And as we walk, we must make the pledge that we shall march ahead. We cannot turn back. There are those who are asking the devotees of civil rights, "When will you be satisfied?" we can never be satisfied as long as our bodies, heavy with the fatigue of travel, cannot gain lodging in the motels of the highways and the hotels of the cities. We cannot be satisfied as long as the Negro's basic mobility is from a smaller ghetto to a larger one. We can never be satisfied as long as a Negro in Mississippi cannot vote and a Negro in New York believes he has nothing for which to vote. No, no, we are not satisfied, and we will not be satisfied until justice rolls down like waters and righteousness like a mighty stream.

I am not unmindful that some of you have come here out of great trials and tribulations. Some of you have come fresh from narrow cells. Some of you have come from areas where your quest for freedom left you battered by the storms of persecution and staggered by the winds of police brutality. You have been the veterans of creative suffering. Continue to work with the faith that unearned suffering is redemptive.

Go back to Mississippi, go back to Alabama, go back to Georgia, go back to Louisiana, go back to the slums and ghettos of our northern cities, knowing that somehow this situation can and will be changed. Let us not wallow in the valley of despair. I say to you today, my friends, that in spite of the difficulties and frustrations of the moment, I still have a dream. It is a dream deeply rooted in the American dream.

I have a dream that one day this nation will rise up and live out the true meaning of its creed: "We hold these truths to be self-evident: that all men are created equal." I have a dream that one day on the red hills of Georgia the sons of former slaves and the sons of former slave owners will be able to sit down together at a table of brotherhood. I have a dream that one day even the state of Mississippi, a desert state, sweltering with the heat of injustice and oppression, will be transformed into an oasis of freedom and justice. I have a dream that my four children will one day live in a nation where they will not be judged by the color of their skin but by the content of their character. I have a dream today.

I have a dream that one day the state of Alabama, whose governor's lips are presently dripping with the words of interposition and nullification, will be transformed into a situation where little black boys and black girls will be able to join hands with little white boys and white girls and walk together as sisters and brothers. I have a dream today. I have a dream that one day every valley shall be exalted, every hill and mountain shall be made low, the rough places will be made plain, and the crooked places will be made straight, and the glory of the Lord shall be revealed, and all flesh shall see it together. This is our hope. This is the faith with which I return to the South. With this faith we will be able to hew out of the mountain of despair a stone of hope. With this faith we will be able to transform the jangling discords of our nation into a beautiful symphony of brotherhood. With this faith we will be able to work together, to pray together, to struggle together, to go to jail together, to stand up for freedom together, knowing that we will be free one day.

This will be the day when all of God's children will be able to sing with a new meaning, "My country, 'tis of thee, sweet land of liberty, of thee I sing. Land where my fathers died, land of the pilgrim's pride, from every mountainside, let freedom ring." And if America is to be a great nation, this must become true. So let freedom ring from the prodigious hilltops of New Hampshire. Let freedom ring from the mighty mountains of New York. Let freedom ring from the heightening Alleghenies of Pennsylvania! Let freedom ring from the snowcapped Rockies of Colorado! Let freedom ring from the curvaceous peaks of California! But not only that; let freedom ring from Stone Mountain of Georgia! Let freedom ring from Lookout Mountain of Tennessee! Let freedom ring from every hill and every molehill of Mississippi. From every mountainside, let freedom ring.

When we let freedom ring, when we let it ring from every village and every hamlet, from every state and every city, we will be able to speed up that day when all of God's children, black men and white men, Jews and Gentiles, Protestants and Catholics, will be able to join hands and sing in the words of the old Negro spiritual, "Free at last! free at last! thank God Almighty, we are free at last!"

Freedom Summer

The marchers sang "we shall overcome someday." In 1964, several hundred civil rights workers were training in Oxford, Ohio. Shortly after the training, three civil rights workers were murdered. This incident is famous as "Freedom Summer." Whites, many of them Jewish, were also involved in the Civil Rights Movement. Over half of the white students who went south to organize voter-registration drives during the Freedom Summer were Jewish (Takaki, 1993).

Bloody Sunday

In 1965, the raid of state troopers to dismantle the peaceful demonstration in Selma, Alabama, turned into violence against the marchers and residents with many casualties. This tragic incident was named "Bloody Sunday."

Non-violence vs. Violence

Non-violence is a very strong and effective weapon. History has shown us that with non-violence we can reach the mountaintop, overcome injustice, and defeat evil. The pioneer of this incredible ideology was Henry David Thoreau, who inspired Mahatma Gandhi and Dr. Martin Luther King, Jr., who later adapted this ideology as part of his famous doctrine.

Violence is generated from bad feelings, which opens a way for evil thinking, and results in wrongdoing and dangerous behaviors. In most cases, the outcome of violence is devastating and beyond control. In today's world of mass media, according to Napoleon Chagnon (Scupin, 2003), we are witnessing numerous accounts of violence and aggression, such as sports brawls, wars, and revolutions. I would also add kidnapping, hostage taking, and the recent brutality of beheading innocent civilians in Iraq by members of terrorist groups.

Dr. Martin Luther King, Jr. believed in non-violence and showed the world that the power of non-violence is enormous. On the contrary, Malcolm X, the militant Black Muslim minister insisted that those who impose violence must be treated with violence. Malcolm X delivered a speech on February 4, 1963 to a crowd at Brown's Chapel in Selma, Alabama, while Dr. King was in jail. In this speech, the radical leader clearly emphasized that other black leaders (referring to himself) do not believe in nonviolent measures. A few weeks later, the radical leader was gun-downed in Harlem, New York (William, 2001).

Dr. Martin Luther King's "I have been to the Mountain Top" Speech

Dr. King delivered his last historic speech known as "I have been to the Mountain Top." the night before his assassination on April 3, 1968, in Memphis, Tennessee. Sanitation workers had an ongoing dispute with white employers. Dr. King's purpose of this speech was to resolve the conflict and mediate without any violence. In this speech Dr. King confessed that he has seen the glory and God has allowed him to reach the mountain top. He declared that he had no fear of anybody and did not think about his life longevity at that time as if he had the feeling that his life was coming to an end.

How Much of the "Dream" Has Become a Reality?

"I say to you today, my friends, that in spite of the difficulties and frustrations of the movement, I still have a dream, it is a dream deeply rooted in the American dream...I have a dream that one day this nation will rise up and live out the true meaning of its creed: [We hold these truths to be self-evident: that all men are created equal]...I have a dream that my four children will one day live in a nation where they will not be judged by the color of their skin but by the content of their character (King, 1963)." These historic words will never be forgotten. We honor them as the best example of the art of public speaking in most communication classes in our academic institutions around the country.

A National Tribute to a Hero

Since 1988 when Martin Luther King day was designated as a national day in the United States, we have been celebrating the legacy of this American Hero every January 20. Most Americans enjoy the MLK holiday, yet some may not know in depth the impact of the 1963 historic speech Dr. King delivered before the Lincoln Memorial in Washington, D.C. With the same token, today, according to Julian Bond, a well-known civil rights activist and a student of MLK, our children in their schools are learning about this hero and his famous dream, but do not know much about his fights on economic injustice, racism, prejudice, and the war in Vietnam. Dr. King received world recognition for his fight against injustice and his humanitarian efforts towards peace and freedom. He won the 1964 Noble Peace Prize.

The Reason for Recognition

The loss of Dr. King was a tragedy to Black America and to all of those who advocate peace, equality, and justice around the world. In many areas of the United States, unrest and tension escalated, and caring and loving people who supported blacks had no choice but to relocate to a different city due to harassment and life threats. A friend of mine whose father was a minister in Cleveland, Ohio remembers those tough days that their family suffered so much because they supported black families. They abandoned their house and most of their belongings and fled the city at midnight after they received a life-threatening note posted on their front door.

King was more than a civil activist or a civil rights leader. Martin Luther King, Jr. was a special figure and he became the cause of salvation, unity, and courage. The movement he came from represented a solidarity that stood up for those who were subject to inequality and was the core of that movement seeking democracy.

Martin Luther King followed the path of world leaders such as Gandhi who is well-known for non-violence. In 1996, Julian Bond praised MLK in this manner (William, 2001): "His courage, his dedication to non-violence, his ability to articulate the longings of Southern blacks to free themselves from domestic apartheid, and his linking of that struggle to the American dream ensured his place in the national consciousness."

A Long Way We Have Traveled, But...

The many decades of struggle for freedom and equality are mostly remembered by those who were involved in the great movement that Rosa Park started and King supported, along with a small circle of older courageous and nationally recognized black civil rights leaders. The genesis of racism, hatred, and seeking justice, is believed to have come from the Holy Land, where Jews and Samaritans had a conflicting environment. This culture of hatred was inherited and reflected in religious ideology. Therefore, civil rights became a religious and spiritual issue as well as a political one. If

Martin Luther King was alive today, he would be somewhat satisfied for all the changes we have gone through to reach the gate of freedom for decades, yet we have not penetrated the fort that is the framework of the "dream" that King's philosophy is structured upon. Although we have devised the Equal Employment Opportunity Act, and enacted Affirmative Action, both of which generated a wide spectrum of acceptance to all cultures including that of African Americans, we have not been able to totally eradicate the discrimination, prejudice, hatred, and inequality of which Martin Luther King dreamed. We celebrated the beginning of the 21st century for what we have achieved so far, yet we still suffer from poverty in the land of wealth, animosity in the land of brotherhood, and experience rejections in the land of opportunity. It is not too late to fulfill the dream (Parvis, 2003).

Some Names to Remember from the Civil Rights Movement era:

Many young Americans do not know that besides Dr. Martin Luther King Jr. and Rosa Parks, thousands of people, black and white, rigorously worked for social justice with the hope that one day black America and other minority groups would become "free at last." History will never forget them. A comprehensive list of these individuals appeared in *Eyes on the Prize* (Williams, 2002). Below are some of the key individuals of the movement in alphabetical order:

Daisy Bates, President of the Arkansas chapter of the NAACP in 1957.

Melba Pattillo Beals, one of the Little Rock Nine, a reporter for NBC, now a writer and a talk show host.

Harry Belafonte, performer, a friend of Dr. Martin Luther King, Jr.

Linda Brown, of *Brown vs. Board of Education*, lives in Topeka, KS.

Oliver Brown, Linda Brown's father, after the 1954 decision, became a pastor in Springfield, MO, and died in 1961.

Thurgood Marshall, special counsel to NAACP, later became an associate justice of the U.S. Supreme Court.

E. D. Nixon, a key organizer of the Montgomery bus boycott, retired from the Alabama NAACP in 1977.

Philip Randolph, the senior civil rights leader who first planned a march on Washington in 1941, with Bayard Rustin, deputy director of the 1963 march.

Wyatt T. Walker, the SCLC chief of staff, 1960-1964, president of the YMCA, New York, now a pastor in Harlem.

Andrew Young, executive VP of the Southern Christian Leadership Conference from 1967-1970, U.S. Ambassador to the U.N., mayor of Atlanta in 1982.

Summary

In the modern history of the United States, the era of civil rights movement (1950s-1960s) is significant due to the fact that America was changed for ever. Many documentaries reveal that diverse people of color especially, black Americans, went through a tough time to be free. The time-line of incidents during the civil rights movement reminds us of the hate crimes based on prejudice, resentment, and bigotry that were having an adverse impact on American society. The Brown v. Board of Education ruling of the Supreme Court put an end to the Plessey v. Ferguson " separate but equal" decision that was practiced from 1896 to 1954 as the law of the land. The Rosa Park incident in 1955 infused the Bus Boycott. Black leaders and supporters of Rosa Parks insisted that Dr. King be the leader of the movement. Initially, he had no desire to be involved, yet he accepted this responsibility. He traveled around the country, presented more than a thousand public speeches, and promoted non-violence as an excellent way to overcome the violence and chaos in many states around the country. In a historic speech in 1963, Dr. King pronounced to Americans and the world his dream that one day blacks and whites will have an equal opportunity to live and work together.

The quest for recognition and equality were made possible through the colossal efforts of many civil rights leaders who worked closely with Dr. King. In his last speech, Dr. King confessed that God had helped him to reach the mountain top. What he accomplished was more valuable than his life longevity as he declared a night before his assassination. The legacy of Dr. King has been carried out by many civil activists to this date. Martin Luther King was more than a hero—

he became the moral conscience for many Americans. We remember Dr. King's legacy by celebrating his birthday of January 15, which is officially observed on a Monday every year.

"A lot of people are waiting for Martin Luther King or Mahatma Gandhi to come back---but they are gone. We are it. It is up to us. It is up to you..."

-Marian Wright Edelman
Founder and Chief Executive Officer of the Children's Defense Fund (CDF)

Test Your Knowledge

Part One: Put T for True and F for False.

1. _____ The Civil Rights Movement in America began as early as 17th century.
2. _____The unrest during the civil rights movement was confined to southern states only.
3. _____ Blacks, who represented almost half of Montgomery's population, did not ride a bus for more than a year.
4. _____ The pioneer of non-violent ideology was Henry David Thoreau.
5. _____Malcolm X followed Gandhi's ideology while Dr. King accepted Thoreau's.
6. _____ Black people's dreams were stronger than white people's hatred.
7. _____ The dark days of suppression and hatred did not stop the decisiveness of those heroes and heroines, black and white.
8. _____ The genesis of racism, hatred, and seeking justice, believed to have come from the Holy Land, where the Jews and Samaritans had a conflicting environment.
9. _____ The radical leader Malcolm X was gun-downed in Harlem, New York by a member of the KKK.
10. _____ The Civil Rights Act was signed into law on July 2, 1964.
11. _____Dr. King did not live long enough to win the Noble Peace Prize.
12. _____The bus boycott incident resulted in MLK being arrested for the first time in his life.

Part Two: Discussion Questions

  a. Why is the Civil Rights Act of July 2, 1964 significant in American history?
  b. How much of MLK's dream has been accomplished and what else do we need to do to carry on where he left off?
  c. From 1896 to 1968, America lived through division, turmoil, and blood shed. Explain the outcome of three significant historical events during this period.

d. What was the driving force behind Dr. King's dream and why did he exclaim that he had reached the mountaintop?

e. The Brown vs. Board of Education ruling of 1954 ended the "separate but equal" law of the land. Why were schools still practicing segregation almost three years after in 1957?

f. Explain the significant differences between Malcolm X and Dr. Martin Luther King.

g. Identify the forces behind the turmoil and terror that resulted after Rosa Parks refused to give up her seat to a white man.

h. Discuss the philosophy of nonviolence pioneers and explain why they believed this philosophy was a strong weapon.

GRUDGE

By Lee B. Erickson

I can't bear the grudge,
the same one you bear.

The energy necessary to bear that burden,
to hold the hate and anger, for me, is needed
elsewhere.

Move forward and beyond. Looking back can only
Cause you to stumble and to keep you from relishing
the joy in life that you so richly deserve.

That burden will hang around your neck for as long
as you let it. That hatred will fill your heart and mind for as long
as you let it.

Only when you forgive and forget will you be truly free of the grudge
you bear.

Chapter 7: Interaction in the Realm of Diversity

"Kind words can be short and easy to speak,
but their echoes are truly endless."
-Mother Teresa
Angel of Mercy, A beloved humanitarian

"I can live for two months on a good compliment."
-Mark Twain
American writer

Objectives

- Distinguish systems and characteristics of culture
- Identify social interactions through Standard Operative Procedures
- Explore the significance of verbal and non-verbal communication
- Analyze the impact of communication on personal relationships
- Examine the importance of communication in cultural diversity
- Compare and contrast the cultural differences in communication
- Discover the benefits of public speaking skills

Introduction

The lack of knowledge and curiosity about other cultures and traditions creates misunderstanding and confusion in social and business interactions. People from different backgrounds have their own cultural characteristics. You don't have to travel around the world to identify these characteristics. In a multicultural society such as the United States, learning about international customs and traditions is quite possible in the workplace, at school, and at worship.

The primary step towards positive interactions with others is the use of proper language. Personalities are revealed through the way we speak and use vocabulary. Intonation plays an important role as well. Some people oftentimes assume that speaking louder to a person whose language is different from us, will help achieve a better dialogue. Even communication between people with the same language and background is not always easy. It requires utilizing the effective methods of good communication which will be discussed later.

We interact with each other through verbal and non-verbal communications. Some cultures use non-verbal communication more than we do here in the United States. Therefore, knowing about the context and different kinds of it will help us to present ourselves well while interacting with others. Doing business in today's global market requires a good understanding of different cultures and styles of communications they represent.

Systems of Culture

Each culture has different methods of interacting with others. These methods represent the ethnic features of that particular culture. The customs each culture possesses is portrayed in the social systems of that culture. These systems are government, economy, religion, and the family institution, that are embraced and shaped by the educational structure of each culture.

Government

The psychological distance that exists between people and their governments around the world demonstrates the way people live, interact with each other, follow the ruling authorities, decide for themselves, or practice a semi-democracy system. In March 2004, some experts on Fox News argued that only 40 to 45 percent of the countries around the world have democracy. With the many human rights violations we see around the world, I personally believe that there are even less—somewhere around 30 to 35 percent! In the early 1980s, the fall of the Berlin Wall and the collapse of communism changed the political spectrum of the world. Yet in the 21st century, we still have some totalitarian regimes. Today, according to the CIA World Factbook (CIA, 2005), there are 26 types of government around the world which include anarchy, dictatorship, totalitarian, monarchy, republic, socialism, and democracy. Among these, theocracy and the Islamic republic are the newest.

Economy

Economies are basically divided into three categories: 1) traditional economies, 2) market economies, and 3) command economies. A traditional economy is based on self-sufficiency, with barter as the form of trade. This type of economy is found in most less developed countries. In a market economy, decisions about goods and services are made primarily by individuals and firms. The best examples of this economy are the United States and Canada. A command economy refers to an economy that is controlled by a central authority which makes most of the decisions. Those countries that practice communism, fascism, and socialism fit into this category (Mastrianna & Hailstones, 1998). Another way of looking at the world economy describes two categories: one a closed system and the other an open system. For example, countries which practice little social mobility are in the first category. On the other hand, an open system economy includes those nations which allow social mobility, achievement and prosperity for their citizens (Lindsey and Beach, 2002).

The United States, Canada, Germany, Sweden, Switzerland and other countries as such are considered open societies. Conversely, Pakistan, Sudan, Somalia, and many similar African, Asian, or Middle Eastern countries are among closed societies. The caste system in India, which is the best example of the inequality and the gap between rich and the poor, portrays the economic stratification in the world.

Religion

In a general sense, religion can be defined as an organized belief system based on certain tenets of faith. In other words, it is a belief in a supreme supernatural force or god. It is important in cultural diversity to respect peoples' values and traditions. Religion is a sensitive issue. No wonder, in most cultures, discussions about religion should be avoided. It is wise not to talk about religion or politics when you interact with people from different cultures, either here in the United States or when visiting another country.

In most cultures, religion does not play a major role in societal development. In other words, the separation of church and state is widely acknowledged. Conversely, in Islamic cultures, religion is the most important system of culture, namely, it embraces the entire way of life. The prominent examples are the Islamic culture of Iranians and other Islamic cultures which have the same tendency for tyranny and dictatorship in the name of Islam. In these cultures, religion overwhelmingly controls the other systems of culture. The Islamic economic system is different from that of the Western world. Some Islamic cultures do not honor interest on loans for instance. That is why Turkey is planning to open an Islamic bank in the Persian Gulf region which would facilitate Islamic countries to do business more easily according to their economic system.

School systems in America are being more considerate about recognizing religious holidays. Not long ago, students from different backgrounds had a hard time revealing their beliefs and traditions to American students. They were teased, bullied, and put on the spot because of their faiths. Nowadays, American school systems are getting more familiar with religious holidays and honor them in their school calendars.

The Major World Religions

Major Religions of the World Ranked by Number of Adherents
Reprinted by permission from www.adherents.com

*Sizes shown are **approximate estimates**, and are here mainly for the purpose of ordering the groups, not providing a definitive number. This list is sociological/statistical in perspective.*

1. Christianity: 2.1 billion
2. Islam: 1.3 billion
3. Secular/Nonreligious/Agnostic/Atheist: 1.1 billion
4. Hinduism: 900 million
5. Chinese tradition religion: 394 million
6. Buddhism: 376 million
7. Primal-indigenous: 300 million
8. African Tradition & Diasporic: 100 million
9. Sikhism: 23 million
10. Juche: 19 million

11. Spiritism: 15 million
12. Judaism: 14 million
13. Baha'i: 7 million
14. Jainism: 4.2 million
15. Shinto: 4 million
16. Cao Dai: 4 million
17. Zoroastrianism: 2.6 million
18. Tenrikyo: 2 million
19. Neo-Paganism: 1 million
20. United-Universalism: 800 thousand
21. Rastafarianism: 600 thousand
22. Scientology: 500 thousand

There are thousands of religions in the world. Clearly, talking about all these religions in detail would be out of the scope of this text. Therefore, I have chosen 6 major religions with a brief description of each. They are: 1) Christianity, 2) Islam, 3) Hinduism, 4) Buddhism, 5) Judaism, and 6) Baha'i.

Christianity: A religion based on the belief of one God, the life and the teachings of Jesus Christ, and the concept of the Holy Trinity. One-third of the world population is Christian. The vast majority of Christians live in Europe and North America, as well as Australia and New Zealand. Christmas is the most important Christian celebration. December 25 is a fixed holy day which denotes the anniversary of the birth of Jesus. The most holy of Christian sacred days is Easter. This holy day commemorates the resurrection of Jesus Christ from death by crucifixion. Good Friday is the Christian remembrance of the crucifixion of Jesus and related events.

Islam: The monotheistic religion based on the doctrine of submission to God and of Muhammad as the chief and last prophet of God. One-fifth of the world population is Muslim and one-fifth of the Muslims live in Southeast Asia. The vast majority of Muslims live in Indonesia (196.3 m) which is a non-Arab country and is located in Southeast Asia. The Middle East is the cluster of Islamic countries with the exception of Israel. However, the Islamic world extends from Europe at large to West, Central, and Southeast Asia.

There are about seven million Muslims in the United States. The majority of Muslims in the United States are African Americans and the rest are either immigrants from Islamic countries or are born here in the U.S. to immigrant parents. The Muslim population in the U.S. should not all be considered as members of the Nation of Islam that is lead by Louis Farrakhan.

The important days in the Islamic faith are: Ramadan (30 days of strict fasting from sunup to sundown; an observance in honor of the first revelations to the Prophet Muhammad); Eid al-Fitr (a three-day celebration at the end of Ramadan); and Eid al-Adha (the end of pilgrimage to Mecca, that is the tenth day of the twelfth month of the Islamic lunar year).

Hinduism: A diverse body of religion, philosophy, and culture native to India, characterized especially by a belief in reincarnation and a supreme being of many forms and natures (Jost, D. A., et al., 1993). Hinduism is the third largest religion in the world. It comprises 13% of the world population.

Buddhism: The teaching of Buddha is that life is permeated with suffering caused by desire, that suffering ceases when desire ceases, and that enlightenment obtained through meditation releases one from desire, suffering, and rebirth (Jost, D. A., et al. (1993). Buddhism is the fourth largest religion in the world. It comprises 6% of the world population. It was founded in Northern India by the Buddha (Sidhartha Gautama). Buddhism is popular across Asia. Since the 13th century it has been the dominant religion in most of Southeast Asia such as Thailand, Burma, Cambodia, and Laos where it is known as Southern Buddhism (Theravada). The Northern Buddhism (Mahayana) is largely found in China, Korea, Tibet, and Mongolia.

Judaism: The monotheistic religion of the Jewish, tracing its origin to Abraham and having its spiritual and ethical principles embodied chiefly in the Bible and the Talmud (Jost, D. A., et al., 1993). In other words, Judaism refers to both ethnicity and religion which is the cultural, religious, and social practices and beliefs of the Jewish people. One percent of the world population is Jewish. Jews are scattered all around the world primarily due to Diaspora, that is, the settling of scattered colonies of Jews outside Palestine after the Babylonian exile. There are about 13 to 14 million Jews in the world. The vast majority of Jews live either in the United States or in Israel (Rich, 2004).

The U.S. Jewish population is estimated to be nearly 6.5 million (U.S. Census, 2004). Israel, in the Middle East, is the state of the Jewish people with a population of 6.2 million. Less than 2 million Jews live in Europe, and the remainder of the world's Jewish population lives in Canada, Latin America, South Africa, Asia, Australia and New Zealand (Rich, 2004).

Jewish holidays, as part of diverse cultural traditions, are respected in America. During the Sabbath, which begins at sundown on Friday evening and ends at nightfall on Saturday, work and other forms of activity are prohibited in the Jewish faith. The celebration of Israel's deliverance from Egyptian repression is known as Passover. Yum Kippur is the holiest day in the Jewish year. On this day Jews fast, pray, and ask for forgiveness from both God and people. Hanukkah, (Chanukah) is an 8 day festival of lights to celebrate the ancient victory of the Maccabees over the Syrians, when the lamp oil was expected to last for only one day but by a miracle of God, lasted for 8 days.

Baha'i: Another religion that is worth mentioning is Baha'i. In 1844 a Persian mystic and visionary called the *Bab* (meaning door to wisdom) predicted a "messiah" who would fulfill all religions. He assumed the name Baha'u'llah which means "The Glory of God." His teachings focused on the principles of universal love, peace, harmony, and brotherhood. *Bab* also gave proclamations of gender equality, ethnic unity, the oneness of all religions which did not please the followers of the only Muslim God. His prophesy aroused hostility among the resident Shiite (Shia) Muslims of Iran who were manipulated by the religious leaders (Mullahs), so he fled to Baghdad (Iraq), then left Iraq for Constantinople (today's Istanbul, Turkey), and finally settled in Ottoman Palestine (today's Israel), where he died in 1892. His legacy was carried out by his son, his grandson and later by the Universal House of Justice to this date. Today, the beautiful monument on Mt. Carmel, near Haifa, Israel, is the Mecca of more than 6 million Baha'is around the world (Coppenger, 2002).

Families

In the United States, mass media has a tremendous impact on the family institution. Television shows often reflect the issues of diversity, such as when Native Americans camped out in the lobby of the White House on the series "The West Wing" seeking better healthcare for reservations; or when an episode of "Whoopi" portrayed a gay marriage happening in Mavis' hotel (along with her many diverse staff, family, and friends); or the many episodes of "Law & Order" that show the abuse and murder of diverse people. Who said that TV can't be educational?

Cultural norms and beliefs establish the foundation of family in each society. There are many ways nations choose to raise a family. Based on traditions and folkloric patterns, people around the world institute their families. The way Americans raise a family may not be acceptable to other cultures and vice-versa. "Society depends on families to carry out certain vital functions, such as socialization of the young and regulation of sexual activity" (Cargan & Ballantine, 2003, p. 159). In some cultures dating, sexual relationships, and having a baby out of wed-lock is forbidden. In western societies none of these are considered a taboo.

Socio-economic conditions play an important role in raising a family and family survival. Poverty in sub-continent India, Sri Lanka, Pakistan, Afghanistan and many African countries is the cause of family dysfunction. When a family institution is under colossal pressures resulting from weakening factors such as a lack of education, lack of discipline, lack of financial stability, and a lack of values, children may be led to immoral aspects of life such as prostitution, theft, drug use and other crimes.

Characteristics of Culture

In addition to the way people do business, select their representatives to political positions, practice their religion, and educate their children, some other concepts are important in their daily practices. These concepts are called characteristics of culture and include but are not limited to time, space, privacy, and territory.

Time

The concept of time differs from culture to culture. In cultures, such as Latin America, process time is practiced rather than clock time. If they make an appointment for 10:30 in the morning it could mean from 10:30 to 10:59 (Laroche, 2003). In other words, showing up is more important than being on time. In western societies 10:30 is 10:30. We, in North America, acknowledge clock time rather than process time. A Native American friend of mine also operates more on process time than clock time. If I ask him to get together around 11:30

he will show up around 11:00 or earlier! By doing this he puts more value and respect on showing up rather than being on time. This does not mean that all Native Americans act like my friend does. In the Middle Eastern culture, process time is more common than clock time. For example, if every body is invited to a dinner party at 7:30 PM, some may show up around 9:30 or even later. To these people, going to the party is the matter of respect, not showing up on time!

Personal Space

Remember when you were a kid you wouldn't let anyone take your space? Each individual likes to have space for privacy, belonging, or a sense of authority. My space is where I operate and I would like to keep it to myself. No one should intrude my space! It is important to respect other people's space and not encroach upon anybody's space. If we do so, we not only show disrespect, but have violated the rights of an individual. Each individual possesses an invisible zone around him/her which is called a "bubble zone." Anthropologist Edward T. Hall calls this "proxemics," which refers to cultural use of space. The bubble zone or comfort zone is the space that each individual puts around himself or herself and prefers not to be intruded upon by anybody. When you unintentionally get too close to people, you may notice that they get uncomfortable and move away. Space issues vary greatly from culture to culture.

Territory

Territory is an area such as home or workplace which a person is responsible as a representative or as an owner to defend against intruders. Obviously, no one wants his/her territory to be encroached upon. Human beings have always been defensive when it comes to territory. This is natural for most living organisms. In cultural diversity, it is important to mention about human territory due to the fact that no one appreciates intrusion from outsiders. The difference between territory and personal space is the actual space that is visible for the former and invisible for the latter. When a neighbor encroaches your territory, even for a yard, you show no tolerance and fight for it until you get it back!

It is important to respect other peoples' territories and seek permission to use that territory. Unfortunately, nationally and globally, we may see where neighborhoods representing different cultural backgrounds become a scene of clashes for gang members when territories have been used by some groups other than those of its own. Accordingly, in some parts of the U. S., blacks may have reservations to enter Italian neighborhoods, or Latinos may hesitate going near Asian territories. This can be seen repeatedly around the world such as India where Hindus have difficulty with Muslims and similarly the unfortunate situation of the Israelis and Palestinians in the Gaza strip and around Jerusalem.

Use of Language

Watch what you say! Be careful of your language! Know your interlocutor (one who takes part in a conversation) before you open your mouth. These are warning statements that most cultural diversity trainers use when educating their clients. Sometimes, we express ourselves without thinking about our words. Our parents always told us: "watch your language!" or "think before you speak." It is always helpful and to our benefit when we rehearse prior to saying something to our friends, colleagues, and other people who have contact with us in our daily life. Improper use of a word can create a huge mess in our world of interaction! One example that received national attention was the use of "niggardly" in 1999. A fellow American, originally from Europe, who was employed by the City of Washington in a meeting with other African American colleagues used that word inadvertently and created a big scandal and fodder for the media to talk about for weeks to come! The user of the word was fired by Mayor Anthony Williams, and a week after was reinstated due to the fact that the word had no link with the "N" word. It meant "miserly" in the dictionary. I am sure the person who used the word learned his lesson not to use such controversial word for the rest of his life.

The media, especially some Hollywood and cable movies do not use proper language. This has influenced many high school and college students. The use of the so called "F" word in the daily conversations of these students is prevalent.

Conflict and Conflict Resolution

In almost all communication books you can find a chapter on conflict and conflict resolution. Conflict, in the minds of many, has a negative connotation. Misunderstanding, disagreement, miscommunication, confrontation, and other face to face provocations as such may fit into the conflict database. The media always uses the word conflict when they refer to the political dispute between two countries. A few examples are the conflict between Israel and Palestine, the U.K. and Northern Ireland conflict, and the Russian and Chechnian conflict. Among these conflicts, Israel and Palestine are amongst the most prominent headline news-makers because this conflict has not yet been resolved. It denotes a battleground that has witnessed thousands of casualties from both sides, due to the suicide bombing of Palestinians and response from Israeli armed forces. The reason for this conflict generates from cultural clashes that have been going on for many years. The root of the conflict can be associated with religion, ideology, viciousness, intrusion of a third party, lack of compromise, and a deep hostility accumulated throughout the years.

A conflict is not always negative. It is often positive, when all energy is shifted towards "good thought, good deed, and good expression." This philosophy is not new to the human race. It goes back to 3500 years ago when Zoroastrianism (one of the oldest monotheist world religions; became the state religion of various Persian empires, until the 7th Century) shed its wisdom over many regions from central Asia to Europe.

There are a number of strategies to resolve a conflict. The most important ones are:

1) avoidance, 2) accommodation, 3) domination, 4) negotiation, and 5) collaboration. In order to achieve effective results, these strategies must be supported with a positive attitude, compromise, cooperation, and avoiding aggravation.

Avoidance—avoidance is synonymous with no confrontation which ends up with no winner or loser. In this case, nothing happens and conflict remains. In some cases avoidance may help prevent further dispute among disagreeable parties.

Accommodation—accommodation involves cooperation and lacks assertiveness. In this approach one party may lose a little by giving in to the other party which may result in a positive future relationship.

Domination—in the domination strategy, one party becomes a dominant power because the struggle is about who must win. Unfortunately, resentment can be created if it is overused. In the 1967 seven-day war between Israel and the Arab coalition led by Egypt,

Israel was the winner. Was the conflict over? Unfortunately not! The conflict has become deeper and deeper.

Negotiation—using the compromising method, involved parties engage in moderate levels of cooperation and assertiveness to achieve an acceptable situation for both. In other words, the loss is minimal and both sides reach a level of agreement which can result in satisfaction for all.

Collaboration—this strategy requires a high level of cooperation and assertiveness. The goals and objective of both parties can be achieved through open communication and high levels of positive attitudes. With positive responses and a high energy level, a ground for resolution can be created with understanding and equal opportunity for conflict resolution. Collaboration consists of four components: understanding and respecting the goals and objectives of each of the parties; assertiveness; creative problem-solving; and confrontation (Alessandra & Hunsaker, 1993).

The Department of Education gives a great deal of attention to delinquency prevention, drugs and violence, and generally anything that creates conflict amongst K-12 students in the United States. One of the subjects that school administrators pay close attention to is conflict and conflict resolution. Our children need to learn how to interact with others, what behaviors should be avoided, and how to make friends rather than enemies in the early stages of their lives.

Communication as a Vital Element of Diversity

Communication as an independent study contributes to many bodies of knowledge. Simply, communication involves sending and receiving messages (DeVito, 1982). In diversity, communication plays an important role due to the fact that interaction with no communication is meaningless. Therefore, one of the key elements of diversity is communication. Generally, communication is presented in two categories: verbal and non-verbal communication. Before we introduce these two divisions, it is necessary to know that there are four skills of communication: 1) speaking, 2) writing, 3) reading, and 4) listening. Being good at all these four skills is not an easy task. Therefore, to be successful in relationships with people from other backgrounds, with a variety of differences, we need to strengthen our capability in these areas of communication.

Verbal Communication

According to a Persian proverb, as long as a man has not spoken, his skills and his flaws are veiled. It is risky how you plan to present yourself. Looking positively, it is to our benefit to speak, see the reactions, get admired or explore the opportunity to improve should there be any defects. Traditional wisdom suggests that you must try otherwise you may not see your mistakes. We need to interact through communicating with our relatives, friends, colleagues, neighbors, coworkers, and other individuals from many backgrounds who deal with us on a daily basis. "Our ability to put our thoughts, feelings, hopes, and dreams into words is the foundation of verbal communication." (Alessandra & Hunsaker, 1993, p. 51). The art of listening, asking questions, and being certain with the help of feedback are valuable parts of verbal communication.

Nonverbal Communication

The reason why nonverbal communication is emphasized in cultural diversity is because it is massively used in many cultures, much more than in North American cultures. Many studies have proven that at least 75 percent of our communication is done via nonverbal components which include body language, appearance, the tone and pace of our voice, eye contact, and other facial expressions. Each of these elements send a certain message and you would be amazed at how common they are in other cultures. Experts believe no matter how good you are in understanding words, being skillful in listening and providing feedback, without the knowledge of nonverbal communication, your communication would not be as effective as you would expect (Alessandra & Hunsaker, 1993).

Nonverbal communication existed before verbal communication developed. Early human beings started to give messages to each other for their daily desires through hand signals, facial expressions, and other body language. Although we enjoy the most advanced tools of verbal communication today, the use of nonverbal communication in many cultures is inevitable.

Nonverbal communication is vastly used in cultures such as Italian, Hispanic, Greek, Middle Eastern, South Asian, and Southeast Asian, to name a few. Even in the United States, nonverbal communication is used on a daily basis in the New York Stock

Exchange (NYSE). Through hand signals, agents in the crowded and noisy NYSE communicate with each other because it is easier and faster than any other tools of communication. Researchers believe that 90 percent of the meaning exchanged between two people is done via nonverbal communication and only 10 percent is transmitted by words. (Alessandra & Hunsaker, 1993) It is important in many cultures to look right in the eyes when doing a business, otherwise you will not be trusted, while in other cultures, to look down at the ground is a sign of respect. Silence is another element of nonverbal communication. For example, in Southwest Asia (Iran, Afghanistan, Pakistan), silence is the sign of satisfaction. You may experience this in other cultures as well.

Styles of Communication: High Context and Low Context

According to the dictionary, context is the part of a text or statement that surrounds a particular word or passage and determines its meaning. It also refers to the circumstances in which an event occurs. It was anthropologist Edward T. Hall who used low context and high context communication styles for the first time. When we communicate with people from different backgrounds, it is helpful to realize what context they belong in, low or high context cultures.

People from high context culture tend to give more attention to the fringe of an event rather than the event itself. In other words, they don't get to the point right away. Nonverbal communication is more common in this category. People from the Far East, Asia, the Middle East, North Africa, southern Europe and Hispanics fit in this category. They are also referred to as polychronic cultures. According to Lionel Laroche (2003) polychronic people tend to do the following:

- do many things simultaneously
- tend to concentrate on the relationships at hand
- welcome interruptions
- take people and information seriously
- tend to change plans according to the needs of the people who are closely related to them
- put less emphasis on privacy and private property—
- objects and information are more readily shared

Low-context communication is the opposite, where the foremost message is in the spoken word. In other words, in this category people do not pay attention to the surroundings of the message rather they tend to focus on the message itself being delivered to the other person. People who fit in this category are called monochronic. According to Lionel Laroche (2003) monochronic people tend to do the following:

- tend to do one thing at a time.
- Tend to concentrate on the task at hand
- Try to avoid interruptions
- Take schedules and deadlines seriously
- Tend to put significant emphasis on privacy and private property

For example, Western Europeans, and North Americans, with the exception of Quebecers and Hispanics, are considered monochronic.

Summary

Each society is based upon strong pillars that hold it firmly together for unity and prosperity. These pillars correspond to government or politics, economy, education, the family institution, and religion which are referred to as the systems of culture. For some nations who believe that there is no separation between church and state (religion and politics), religion is the key to every lock. They do what religion dictates, from kinship to business transactions, to domestic or foreign policies. It is important to know the different styles of politics, economics, family relationships, and educational norms of the cultures of the world.

Cultural uniqueness helps us realize how cultures function when they associate with cultures different from theirs. In dealing with other cultures either domestic or international, it is less confusing when you understand the different concepts of time and styles of communication. People may have clock time or process time. In clock time, you are more precise with seconds and minutes. In process time, more emphasis is given to the event not the arrival time. In North American style, low context refers to how people focus on the word spoken and stick to the point of discussion or the context. Conversely, high context cultures are dealing with peripheral components rather than the core or focal point. Comparing and contrasting these two communication styles reveal that Westerners are monochronic or low-context as opposed to the Eastern cultures that fall into polichronic or high-context cultures. It should also be noted that there's always exceptions. For example, in North American culture you may find

Quebecers and Hispanics who are considered a high context group. In cultural diversity, non-verbal communication has an important place. Many cultures use non-verbal communication more than verbal communication. People communicate with facial expressions, eye contact, body language, and signals. Communication is a key element in cultural diversity. It not only leads us to effective interactions with people from different backgrounds, we benefit from it by resolving our conflicts through negotiation, assertiveness, and compromise. We turn around our negative attitudes into positive responses and collaboration.

Test Your Knowledge

Part One: Discussion Questions

1. What do we mean by the psychological distance between people and governments?
2. Why do some cultures revolve everything around their religions?
3. To what extent should governments interfere with family values and morality?
4. Recently, Bill Cosby was outspoken about how black families were neglecting to properly bring up and educate their offspring. Why were some black families upset about his remarks?
5. It has been argued that some TV and radio programs and Hollywood movies are hazardous to our family institutions. What should people do to ban shows such as the Howard Stern show?
6. Why do some human rights activists think that we should encourage immigrants such as Hispanics (the majority ethnic group) to use their native languages in the U.S.? How may this idea impact effective communication with people from different backgrounds?

Part Two: Fill in the blanks:

1. Christian remembrance of the crucifixion of Jesus and related events is called....................
2. ....is the most holy of Christian sacred days.
3. During ....which begins on Friday evening and ends at nightfall on Saturday, work and other forms of activity are prohibited in the Jewish faith.
4. The celebration of Israel's deliverance from Egyptian bondage is called.........................
5. The holiest day in the Jewish year is......................This day is marked by fasting and prayer, as Jews ask forgiveness from both God and people,
6. The ninth month in the Islamic calendar which entails 30 days of strict fasting from sunup to sundown is known

as………………………………..This observance is in honor of the first revelations to the Prophet Muhammad.

7. Eid al-Adha is the most important feast of Islam that is celebrated on the end of ………………………………………on the tenth day of the twelfth Islamic month.

8. The anniversary of the birth of the Bab (Bahaullah), is the herald of the new age for Baha'is. The Shrine of the Bab in…………………………..is part of the World Center of the Baha'i faith.

9. ----------------------is the fourth largest religion in the world. It was founded in Northern India. One fundamental belief of this faith involves reincarnation.

10. Vaidika Dharma or "religion of the Vedas" is referred to as……………………This religion is vastly practiced in India.

11. ………………………..is an 8 day festival of lights to celebrate the ancient victory of the Maccabees over the Syrians.

12. The vast majority of Muslims (196.3 m) live in……………..which is a non-Arab country and is located in South East Asia.

"Behavior is what a man does, not what he thinks, feels, or believes."

-*Emily Dickinson*
American lyrical poet

"Conflict is the gadfly of thought. It stirs us to observation and memory. It instigates to invention. It shocks us out of sheep-like passivity, and sets us at noting and contriving."

-*John Dewey*
American philosopher and educator

"We could have no communication whatever with our surroundings if they were absolutely foreign to us. Man is reaping success every day, and that shows there is a rational connection between him and nature, for we never can make anything our own except that which is truly related to us."

-*Rabindranath Tagor*
Indian Poet and Philosopher

Chapter 8: Personal Conduct

"If you are good to the others, you would be great to yourself."

-Benjamin Franklin
American inventor, philosopher, and writer

"Whatever is disagreeable to yourself do not do unto others."

-Zoroastrianism

"Good people proceed while considering what is best for others is best for themselves."

-Hinduism

"For our discussion is about no ordinary matter, but the right way to conduct our lives."

-from the Republic of Plato

Objectives

- Refurbish your social conduct by demystifying good human behavior
- Identify negative thoughts and replace them with positive attitudes
- Explore the words of wisdom that have shed a light over humanity
- Analyze the ramifications we may encounter from our uncivilized conduct
- Utilize critical thinking to diminish ignorance and evil thoughts
- Discover the golden rule which many ancient philosophies have believed in
- Examine the advantage of positive energy and high morale in human relations

Introduction

Most people would agree that thoughtful behavior, manners, and common decency are in short supply in today's society. Furthermore, in our busy daily lives of multitasking and cyberspace we simply forget to use our manners which sometimes creates tension and hard-feelings. To improve the quality of our lives we need to be more familiar with good manners and behaviors. Recently, professor P.M. Forni, the cofounder of the Johns Hopkins Civility Project, in his book *Choosing Civility,* identified 25 rules that are most fundamental for connecting effectively and joyfully with others. I found them very helpful as a conduit to cultural diversity education. It is a fundamental approach to teachers' education as well, if we include civility and ethics in the curriculum of those who are planning to become secondary education teachers. As soon as we implement this in the secondary education programs around the country we shall start to see positive results. For the last two decades, the Department of Education has spent millions of dollars on research and studies to prevent delinquency, the use of drugs and violence, and the uncivilized conduct of students around the country. We would curtail huge spending on such studies if we educate our future teachers to promote thoughtful behavior and common decency in the schools and garner the cooperation of parents.

Civility

Almost every culture and civilization has clearly emphasized personal conduct and behavior. Undoubtedly, civility belongs in the realm of ethics. In this respect, one can find a true meaning of morality and the dexterity of human life in ancient wisdom. Zoroastrians believed in the essentials of virtue and based their life values on three principles: 1) good expressions, 2) good deeds, and 3) good thoughts.

Civility is defined in many ways; some see it as being a Good Samaritan, some relate it to honesty and truth, one may believe it as love for neighbors, and perhaps it is a collection of all these good things. Civility is complex, with many attributes. What ever civility might be, it has to deal with courtesy, politeness, and good manners (Forni, 2002).

George Washington left a collection of 110 rules of civility. They are worth reading and should be used in daily life. On etiquette and respect he expresses that "Every action done in company, ought to be with some sign of respect to those that are present." Parents in most cultures teach their offspring how to acknowledge others and pay respect while in the company of other people. The great American writer Ralph Waldo Emerson states that: "We must be as courteous to a man as we are to a picture, which we are willing to give the advantage of a good light." We make every effort to exhibit a picture at home or in a gallery, in the best light. Human beings deserve such attention too.

Besides what we learn from our parents, there are always opportunities to learn from other people who we interact with on a daily basis—from our neighborhood, our schools, and place of work.

Indeed civility and ethics have a direct link with cultural diversity. In order to do well in a multicultural society we must follow the rules of civility that have been recommended by many great individuals. The following rules of civility are selected for diversity purposes from *Choosing Civility* (Forni, 2002):

1) pay attention, 2) listen, 3) speak kindly, 4) think the best, 5) be inclusive, 6) be agreeable, 7) assert yourself, 8) acknowledge others, 9) mind your body, 10) respect other's opinions, 11) respect other people's space, 12) respect even a subtle "No," 13) respect other people's time, 14) keep it down and reconsider silence, 15) apologize earnestly and thoughtfully, 16) avoid personal questions, 17) be a considerate guest

In our major cities, especially in New York, I noticed that civility is being reminded to the general public by posting signs in different places saying: "Courtesy is contagious." The truth to this message is observed by all of us in our daily lives. People are followers regardless. In order to be a good citizen we must choose to utilize good manners and rest assure that others will follow. As a good citizen we must make ourselves useful for our fellow citizens. Ralph Waldo Emerson says: "Make yourself necessary to someone." If every human being thinks and does the way advised by Emerson our world would be a nicer place to live. "I will look upon many human contacts today with real understanding. I am here by design" (Casey & Vanceburg, 1985).

Magic words

When you were little, didn't your parents say "say the magic words and may be you'll get what you want?" It never hurts to say please, thank you, and acknowledge that you are sorry. These "magic words" are tasteful ingredients of good relationships and social interactions. Have you ever noticed that people get angry with each other, do not communicate for a number of weeks, or end their relationships simply because neither party will make an effort to say that they were wrong and need to reconnect with a plain apology.

A few years ago, Donald McCullough, president of the San Francisco Theological Seminary, pastor and professor of theology wrote a book called *Say Please, Say Thank You: The Respect We Owe One Another*. In this book he reminds parents how important it is to make magic words a habit of children from the earliest stages of life. These words are instrumental at home, at work, and in public places. It is remarkably important to use magic words in our personal conduct, and in intimate or social relationships, due to the fact that they save us from resentment, hard feelings, and stress.

Remind youngsters to use polite words to help them express themselves in the company of elders and other people they should respect. Indeed, it becomes a habit that benefits everybody in business and social conversations. My observations from other cultures and visiting various countries always remind me that the words we use present our personalities and social qualities. When in England, I noticed that the failure to use magic words are very insulting to people. The British are very adamant about daily interactions supported by kind words. Native American chiefs are famous in expressing quality of life through interacting with other people especially elders. In community gatherings, words of wisdom were the basis of the education of tribal people.

In short, using magic words add benefits to our relationships with our siblings, parents, friends, and co-workers. Even in the public and the interacting with people who we meet for the first time, civility encourages us to be conscientious of the words we use. By using magic words we encourage others to do the same.

Respect

One of the factors in cultural diversity that binds us together is respect. Respect comes in many forms. Respect other people if you want to be respected. It does not have to follow a certain rule when it comes to respect. A few centuries ago people were respected according to their class or socio-economic status. Even in modern time *respect* is associated with certain groups in places where classism is practiced. By every word we say or every action we perform we can express our respect or lack of respect for others. When someone invites us to a gathering, party, wedding, or any occasion as such we must respond in a timely manner to acknowledge the invitation. Obviously, we are being respected by the invitation and it deserves immediate attention. We ought to respect people for who they are regardless of their national origins and other personal specifications. It is vitally important to *R.S.V.P.* to an invitation upon receipt. In communication, respect plays an important role. Listening carefully, not interrupting while someone else is talking, answering questions, and paying attention are all signs of respect for other people. The following attributes are advantageous in our relationships with others from different backgrounds:

- Respect people for who they are not where they come from
- Respect others' opinions
- Respect others' time
- Respects others' space
- Respect others' territory
- Respect others' privacy
- Respect others' orientations
- Respect others' religions
- Respect others' political affiliations

The list can go on endlessly. The result of being respectful unconditionally will help us to be better individuals and enjoy the quality of life to the fullest.

Acceptance

With a glance at the above mentioned list, one can easily find out that communication is one of the key words in civility. Our verbal and non-verbal communications play important roles in dealing with people. The rules of conduct suggest that we must be a good communicator. This is the primary tool in being a good citizen. Once we overcome our negative attitudes and replace them with positive thoughts we step in the realm of acceptance. In order to accept others one should be prejudice free and accept people for who they are not where they are from. The most disturbing act in diversity is the lack of acceptance. Civility teaches us how to live together with no tension and hard feelings. There is no reason to be reluctant and treat people with ignorance. With acceptance we open the door to understanding. This will help us to be concerned for people more than we are for ourselves—and this is the beginning of the journey to reach love and affection.

Inclusion

Inclusion simply means the act of including or the state of being included. Open-mindedness, tolerance, and simple kindness are the primary tools for someone to use when faced with inclusion at work, in the neighborhood, and anywhere with a diverse population. In places of worship everywhere around the world, people from any background are welcomed. Doors are open to everyone in a sanctuary regardless of color, size, shape, faith, orientation and the like. This ideology can help us to respect and be considerate.

Today, most organizations make efforts to turn their working environment into a better place for productivity, teamwork, respect, and sharing ideas. By including and inviting others into your realm of activity you flash your green light, demonstrating your willingness to care and share with no reservation.

Often time expatriates working and living in the United Sates experience exclusion at work. Those individuals with different faiths and styles of life need to be respected for who they are. The lack of knowledge about people of different faiths and life styles create circumstances that may be damaging in social environments, especially in the workplace. The more we learn about different cultures the better we can get along with them. Learning about other people's faiths helps us to realize that while they have different styles of worship which may look unusual to us, they are still human beings who are basically the same as us. Jews, Muslims, Hindus, Buddhists, and Baha'is are people of faith who live and work with the majority of the population in the U.S. who are Christians of different denominations. Muslims have to pray five times a day of which one time may fall into the working hours around noon time. Imagine in your workplace a person is finding a clean, calm, and traffic free corner where he or she can pray for a few minutes and perform their daily dues to their God (Allah) whom they worship. What would be your reaction? If you have no knowledge about the Muslim faith you would find this posturing weird, unrealistic, and out of whack.

Inclusion embraces many attributes. It is not only about religion or philosophy, it brings a lot of norms under its umbrella. In a simple definition, inclusion means to welcome everybody to your circle and let them feel at home. When at work, inclusion is about acknowledging your co-workers regardless of their backgrounds. In short, inclusion incorporates a simple greeting, remembering names, sharing your thoughts and ideas, listening, and engaging in an emphatic communication.

Positive Attitude

In recent years, many writers and promotional speakers have emphasized the value of positive thinking, positive moods, and positive attitudes. Lynn Grabhorn the author of *Excuse Me, Your Life is Waiting,* with straight-forward language and simple explanations insists that our lives are in trouble without positive thinking. By introducing the astonishing power of feelings she encourages us to pump out negative energy from our bodies and replace them with a positive battery. The result is astonishing. For some people it seems to be a difficult task to dissociate with negative thoughts. Grabhorn suggests that you get the garbage out of your body and revitalize it with the positive energy that is the potential force for storing good feelings and being defiant of crabby moods (Grabhorn, 2000).

The benefits of positive thinking and having no negative attitudes prevail in many ways. By overcoming negative thoughts, we reach the opportunity to be in peace, having clear thinking, and experience happiness. Compare and contrast those who are negative and those who are positive. Clearly, we find success and a joy of life in those who do not let negativity enter their minds. We do it to ourselves—and we must have acquired it from a source, it could be our cultural norms, or the influence of someone else. The ability to get negativity out of our minds is an art which needs to be learned and practiced until it becomes a natural habit.

The benefits of positive thinking embrace our entire being as a human. The impact of positive thinking in every aspect of life generates a driving force for moving forward and experiencing success. The end result is happiness that plays a defiant role against self- destruction.

Positive thinking has amazing results. Among the many wonderful statements said about positive thinking this anonymous quote grabbed my attention: "The positive thinker sees the invisible, feels the intangible, and achieves the impossible."

For creating positive thinking, we need to have positive energy by not focusing on our insecurity but on our strengths. This is what you should say to yourself: "I am going to feel and trust the positive energy inside me. I'm going to claim my full power" (Orloff, 2004, p.266). This selective power will move you forward and make you ready to confront with and overwhelm the negative reservoir inside you.

Summary

From time to time we need to remind ourselves how to interact with people in proper ways. We need to find out how we should communicate with others without creating hard feelings and resentment. Good personal conduct is significant in human relations, especially in a diverse environment. Today, many believe that we are in a short supply of good conduct and civility. Therefore, it is important to review the rules of civility and use them as they become necessary.

Civility is a complex concept with so many attributes. The easy way to grasp it is to begin with good manners, politeness, and consideration. Many philosophers have emphasized civility and social conducts. Almost all religions have talked about the rules of civility. You may also find them in books and works of philosophy.

About 3500 years ago, in Persia (today's Iran), located in southwest Asia, the rules of civility and human morality were practiced by Zoroastrians. Three famous rules of Zoroastrian civility were Good Expressions, Good Deeds, and Good Thoughts.

Collectively, almost all ancient civilizations expressed the golden rule as "Do unto others as you would have others do unto you." It's a simple expression with colossal meaning. It is necessary for all of us to invest in civility and good manners since we are told that choosing civility is a good human asset that should not be kept in short supply.

In our social conduct and interaction with people from numerous backgrounds we ought to use the magic words, have respect for others, include other people in our realm with open arms, accept people for who they are, and fill our empty filing cabinets with positive attitudes. We need to remind ourselves, once in a while, that good personal conduct is the passport to visit other people's social domain with peace and comfort.

Test Your Knowledge

Part One: Learning from quotations.

Instruction: Provide three examples for each of the following famous quotes.

1. George Washington once said "Every action does in company, ought to be with some sign of respect to those that are present."
   a...
   ....b...
   ....c.....................
   ....
   ......

2. According to Ralph Waldo Emerson "We must be as courteous to a man as we are to a picture, which we are willing to give the advantage of a good light."
   a...
   ....
   b...
  c
   ....
   ....

3. Mark Twain said: "I can live for two months on a good compliment."
   a...
   ....
   b...
   ....c...
   ....

4. Gilbert Chesterton reminds us that "Acceptance is the truest kinship with humanity."
   a...
   ....
   b...
   c...

5. The British philosopher Bertrand Russell advises us that "Nobody gossips about other people's secret virtues."
   a...
   b...
   c...

Part Two: Discussion Questions

1. How does civility relate to cultural diversity?
2. Almost all holy books insist you love your neighbors. My neighbor believes he is a good Christian. Why does he dislike people of color?
3. Should common decency, manners, and social behavior be subjects of study in the U.S. schools? Why?
4. How does the "golden rule" apply to your daily life? What can you do to restock the short supply of civility and ethics?
5. What would be your reaction to a colleague or classmate from a different background if he or she does not associate with you?
6. How would you discuss your feelings with your parents when you realize they are prejudiced and ignorant?
7. What is your perception of the phrase: "courtesy is contagious."
8. How does good communication relate to the rules of conduct?
 9. What are the advantages of being positive?
10. How can you wipe out the negative thoughts from your mind and heart?
 11.How would you confront a police officer if he used profanity while communicating with you?

UNTITLED
By Lee B. Erickson

Last night I dreamed you were me.
You could see my world from my perspective
and you cried because you couldn't believe
all the pain and hatred and misunderstanding
that you people put on my people.

Two nights ago I dreamed you were the devil.
You didn't believe anything different from what
you believe now. You judged and hated
until my people had no choice but give up
their spirits. Spirits created by our God.

Tonight I sit on my bed, pondering sleep and dreams.
If I had a choice, I'd dream it like it used to be
when we would write and ponder life and love,
good friends challenging the boundaries of our thinking.
When you had no absolutes to block me from your shore.

PART THREE

**Power Distance
And Human Sensitivity**

Chapter 9: Diversity and Human Rights

"America did not invent human rights. In a very real sense, it is the other way around. Human rights invented America."

-President Jimmy Carter
2002 Nobel Peace Prize Laureate

Objectives

- Comprehend the concept of human rights at home and abroad
- Delve into the characteristics of human rights in the world of diversity
- Discover domestic and international human rights violations
- Analyze the role of the United Nations vis-à-vis human rights
- Justify the Universal Declaration of Human Rights (UDHR)
- Identify the impact of terrorism on diversity and human rights
- Examine the advantage of human rights commissions in the U.S.
- Discuss immigration issues with regard to diversity and human rights

Introduction

The world's governments became familiar with human rights when the Universal Declaration of Human Rights (UDHR) was put together in 1948. After more than five decades, many people around the world still have no clue what human rights are all about. Human rights are violated in more than 40 percent of the world's nations and the United Nations remains an entity with no absolute power to confront dictators and tyrants who rule their people with oppression and inhumane behaviors.

In the western world where democracy reigns, people have opportunities to raise their voices and reduce the gap between citizens and governments. This gap that is identified as psychological distance creates substantial domination and cruelty as it grows wider and deeper. The rights of people around the world, especially women and children, are violated in the name of religion, political philosophy, or friendship with super powers. All these attributes are associated with totalitarianism and absolute power that rulers enjoy with callous tyranny.

In the United States, Europe, and other parts of the world, after the tragedy of 9/11, human rights were violated in the name of national security. People from the Middle East, North Africa, and Asia were scrutinized by security personnel in many public arenas, especially the airports. In our diverse nation where more than 165 different nationalities and cultures live and work together, controlling and maintaining peace and freedom are not easy tasks as we need to be vigilant for any suspicious activities. Now the dominant majority is watchful and sensitive to foreign appearances. Accordingly, human rights became an even more important issue as we strive to embrace diversity and enhance our conviviality.

The Basics of Human Rights

On December 10, 1948, the General Assembly (consisting of delegates from 58 countries—socialist countries, Saudi Arabia, and South Africa were absent) adopted the draft of the "International Declaration of Human Rights" in Paris (Ippoliti, 2004). The outcome of this historic assembly was 30 articles which became well-known to the world as the Universal Declaration of Human Rights (UDHR). Eleanor and Franklin Roosevelt were instrumental in the drafting of the new 'second Bill of Rights,' which declared civil-political and economic-social rights to be universal and indivisible.

For more than half a century, these articles have been helpful for United Nations professionals and human rights advocates, although human rights have never been fully respected and protected around the world. The universal declaration embraces some basic principles that support the 30 articles (see appendix C).

For people around the world, it is vital to understand the principles of human rights and relate them to their real-life situations. These principles are: equality, universality, non-discrimination, indivisibility, interdependence, and responsibility (Flowers, et al., 2000).

The Definition of Human Rights

In a general sense, human rights are the legal, political, and moral claims to conditions necessary for the well-being of individuals. In a philosophical realm, human rights are based on the concepts of human dignity and nondiscrimination among individuals. To view this legally, human rights are based on the national constitution, laws, and international treaties that compel governments to act in certain ways in relation to individuals under their authority.

According to natural law theorists, human rights are considered moral rights or ethical rights while legal positivists pinpoint fundamental rights they find in the law. Interestingly enough, these arguments whether grounded in natural law or legal positivism have become accepted as part of customary international law. It is appropriate to note that the U.S. constitution enjoyed natural law and natural rights. The "Declaration of Independence" is the most prominent example of natural rights stated by our founding father Thomas Jefferson. This respected document affirms that: "We hold these truths to be self-evident, that all men are created equal, that they were endowed by their Creator with certain inalienable Rights, that among Men, deriving their just powers from the consent of the governed" (Encyclopedia Britannica, 2005). And therefore from this natural law approach one can claim that human rights result from the fact of being human and are therefore inherent in individuals.

A Basic Human Right: The Right to Own Property (Article 17)

John Locke, the British philosopher, was the first who emphasized that one of the fundamental human rights was the right to own property, from which later civil and political rights were generated giving birth to Article 17 of the Universal Declaration of Human Rights, the "Right to Own Property." This article specifies that: 1) Everyone has the right to own property alone as well as in association with others, and 2) No one shall be arbitrarily deprived of his property. The United States of America is blessed with an abundance of natural resources, technological advances, wealth, and freedom. Millions of our fellow citizens are either homeless, low-income renters, or have no initial support or resources for affordable housing.

Human Rights Commissions, support for the humanitarian intentions of communities, and civil organizations whose constant efforts strive for affordable housing will bring the hope of life and security to millions of citizens in this country.

Human Rights and Immigration

Immigration has always been a controversial issue in the United States. In recent years, especially after September 11, and each time we are embroiled in elections, talk about immigration increases. There are so many myths about illegal immigration, yet we should bear in mind that for every myth there may be indeed a fact. Conventional wisdom seeks the fact and throws away the myth. With the flux of immigrants comes cultural diversity and for many, confusion and misperceptions.

The Department of Justice and the Immigration and Naturalization Services (INS) oversee the affairs of legal aliens in the U.S. In each state there's an INS office which normally provides services for legal immigrants. In major areas of the United States where many immigrants reside incidents pertaining to human rights violations have been evident.

Myths and Facts

There so many myths and facts about immigrants these days. According to Minnesota Advocates for Human Rights (mnadvocates.org, 2004) a myth says that: "Most immigrants to the United States are illegal, undocumented aliens who come only for economic reasons." The fact is: based on INS records, 849,807 immigrants were legally admitted to our country in the year 2000. The fact of the matter is that economics was a role player in these arrivals, but more importantly family, secured jobs, and freedom, in particular, are more significant factors influencing these people's decisions to leave their homeland. The majority of Americans can not understand how difficult it is to leave your birthplace, relatives, friends, culture, and the accustomed environment and flee to a country where you have to start from scratch, bear strange looks and some animosity, accept low-paying jobs, and be deprived from the many amenities of life that are readily available for others. Recent data reveals that, among immigrants who came to this country in 2000, 69% arrived to be reunited with their immediate family members, 13% came to fill the jobs no U.S. worker was willing or available to do, and 8% were refugees who fled their countries due to persecution and found the U.S. as a land of safety and freedom. "Like generations of immigrants before them, these immigrants came to this country looking for a better life, and their energy and ideas enrich all our communities." (mnadvocates.org, 2004)

Immigrants and the Make up of Diversity

There's much to say about immigrants in the land of immigrants. It is so important that younger generations realize that America is built upon immigrants who came from many countries in the world and for centuries the exodus of diverse people to the promised land (the U.S.A.) never stopped and continues to this day. With the laws on legal immigration and the pressure of opponents to control illegal immigration, the country has not witnessed any mass emigration in recent years with the exception of Hmong refugees and the period of 1992-2000 which legally brought more than 1.5 million people to the United States from all over the world.

Many Americans assume that immigrants are only residing in Texas or California. As a surprise to the majority who are oblivious about the make up of immigrants in the country, this is not the case. Minnesota is an example, where there are at least 100 ethnic groups of which the majority reside in the greater Twin Cities (Minneapolis-St. Paul). This state is one of the fastest-growing states in the union leading in business, industry, and education. Minnesota is the second largest area of the country for the Hmong population, after California, with more than 60,000 Hmongs who began leaving refugee camps in Thailand (from 1975 to 2004) for the United States with the help from the U.S. government and churches.

USA Today (2005) in its report "America the Diverse" featured 11 places in the United States. The summary of this report is as follows:

1. **Dearborn, a suburb of Detroit, Michigan** is the largest Middle Eastern community in America. It is called the Arab-American Capital. Nearly half a million Arabs live in this area. People from the

Arabian countries of the Middle East immigrated to the Detroit area as early as 19th century.

2. **Minneapolis-St. Paul** is the home of more than 60,000 Hmong who began coming to Minnesota some 30 years ago after the end of Vietnam War. The Hmong population in Minnesota is mainly concentrated in St. Paul where they have established more than 250 businesses fostering the revitalization of an urban neighborhood. There are about 1.1 million Hmong immigrants from Southeast Asia living in the U.S.

3. **Holmes County area, in eastern Ohio**, is the home to nearly 40,000 Amish which is considered the largest Amish enclave in the country. At the Amish and Mennonite Heritage Center you can get a sense of the religion and by touring Schrock's Amish Farm
you have a chance to see how a working farm operates.

4. **Chicago** is the "Second City" to the Polish people after Warsaw, Poland. More than a million Polish live in the Chicago area. From 1851 to 1920, Chicago became the largest Polish immigration community in the world. The impact of the Polish culture and heritage is quite prevalent in Chicago. The Taste of Polonia festival is a very famous festivity each Labor Day!

5. **Cajun County of Louisiana,** is the home of French-speaking Acadians. They came to southwestern Louisiana in late 18th century after the English drove them from Canada. In the fertile land of New Iberia and 22 counties of Cajun Country, the culture was reshaped by valuing families, good music, and great food through planting, ranching, and respecting nature.

6. **Barrio Historico, in Tucson, Arizona** is famous for 150 adobe row houses. This largest collection of traditional Sonoran architecture in the country is located in downtown Barrio Historico. Tucson as a Spanish colonial outpost became part of the United States after Mexico became independent in 1821. Brightly colored adobes are part of the barrio's attraction which portray a magnificent place to celebrate a part of Mexican immigrants heritage and contribution to American culture.

7. **Harlem in New York City** is famous not only to Americans but to the entire world. It has acquired many names and meanings throughout the history of America. It is called the cultural capital of Black America. Quite a few famous people such as W.E.B. Du Bois, Langston Hughes, and Zora Neale have introduced it to the world. To food lovers, it is the home of Creole-fusion restaurants and down-

home soul kitchens; and to Jazz lovers it is known for the historic places where Jazz music in America flourished.

8. **Little Havana, in Miami, Florida** is the Cuba of America. After the 1959, Castro revolution, Cuban émigrés colonized the area. Little Havana is famous for the Calle Ocho festival which brings more than a million people each year on the last Friday of March to the biggest Hispanic street party. This remarkable diversity celebration is a unique festival which attracts thousands of vendors, people in costume, merengue bands, and the longest conga line. Little Havana, in Miami, is a point of attraction for many U.S. and foreign tourists. It's politically, economically, and socially desirable!

9. **Los Angeles, California** is an extraordinary example of a diverse place in America. Many people from different backgrounds and ethnicities reside in L.A. Japanese Americans have their own "Little Tokyo" which is a cultural hub of L.A. with many points of attractions including restaurants, shops, traditional gardens, and Buddhist temples. Los Angeles has been called "Tehrangeles" for the reason that at least half a million Iranians live and work in the L.A. area. The Westwood area is the hub of the Iranian culture with many shops and restaurants.

10. **Brighton Beach, Brooklyn, N.Y.** became a seaside resort and the nation's largest Russian Jewish community in the Victorian age. In 1920s it was no longer as fashionable as it used to be but then later it was filled with Eastern Europeans who fled after WWI. In the late 1970s a second wave of immigration hit the place. This time around, tens of thousand of immigrants came from the former Soviet Union (today's Russia). Today, Brighton Beach, Brooklyn is once again a bustling, thriving area.

11. **Cherokee Nation in Tahlequah, OK** was formed in 1838. The tribal people built all the necessary citadel amenities for their families, published a bilingual newspaper, and enacted a representative government 70 years before Okalahoma gained statehood. Today, Tahlequah is the political, economical, and cultural capital of both the Cherokee Nation, the nation's largest tribe (729,533), and the United Keetoowah Band.

Blending with the Mainstream

Our sisters and brothers from different backgrounds do realize that they are part of the American community, and they are trying their best to blend with mainstream America by improving their English, the legal language of our land. Other immigrants who came to this country from all parts of Europe and Asia did not forget their backgrounds, yet were also able to assimilate themselves to mainstream America. This land of freedom and opportunity respects all religions, languages, ideas, and traditions. We acknowledge cultural diversity and appreciate the traditions of other lands, arts, food, etc.— in fact, we welcome them!

Women and the Violation of Human Rights

There used to be an advertising slogan aimed at women that stated: "You've come a long way…!" And while that may be true in some aspects, there's still a long way to go to protect the human rights of women. Amongst all human rights issues, the violation of women's rights has recently been the center of attention not only in local human rights groups, but in many human rights organizations around the world. Women in North America have not been subjected to the same human rights violations, torture, mutilation, and horrible crimes as in other parts of the world. However, they are still the victims of sexual assaults, battering, discrimination and terrible domestic crimes. For years, the issue of violence against women was not spoken of, it was a big, ugly, shameful secret that no one wanted to acknowledge. Now is the time to take that secret out of the proverbial closet and deal with it. Recently, Lifetime Television for Women had a day of programming aimed at creating awareness of the violence against women. These shows depicted rape, abuse, murder, and other crimes against women. Although many women are already aware of the problems it will be useful that the role of society and the media empowers some women to take action; but how many abusers got the message? How do we reach the abusers while taking care of the victims and preventing future incidents?

Women and Human Rights around the World

In November, 2002, in Washington, D.C., Parvin Darabi delivered a speech on oppression in the Islamic Republic of Iran. She expressed that in Iran under the Islamic regime "A woman cannot travel, work, go to college, join organizations, visit her friends and relatives without her father or husband's permission." Ms. Darabi organized a foundation in memory of her sister Dr. Homa Darabi who set herself on fire in a Tehran's square protesting the brutality of the regime shooting to death an innocent girl for wearing lipstick in public.

In 2003, the Noble Peace Prize was awarded to Shirin Ebadi, a lawyer from Iran. Shirin Ebadi's many years of great efforts in advocating human rights in Iran, especially women and children's rights, were unprecedented in the suppressed society of Iran. Her humanitarian hard work attracted the attention of Oslo judges from among 150 applicants from all over the world. It was a great victory for women around the world.

Shirin Ebadi's statements have been quoted in many publications since 2003. She expresses herself on cultural diversity and human rights as follows:

> If the 21st century wishes to free itself from the cycle of violence, acts of terror and war, and avoid the repetition of the 20th century – that most disaster - ridden century of humankind; there is no other way, except by understanding and putting into practice every human right for all mankind, irrespective of race, gender, faith, nationality or social status.

Recent events have galvanized us to pay attention to the many victims in the brutal, sadistic and dysfunctional societies around the world, particularly in southwest Asia. Afghani women, for example, have experienced unbelievable tragedies, worse than those of the dark ages. The Revolutionary Association of the Women of Afghanistan (RAWA), and American organizations such as the Afghan Women's Mission in Pasadena, California, are fighting to save these women from brutal atrocities.

Dr. Sima Samar, a 2001 John Humphrey Freedom Award recipient, is an Afghani physician who fought for women's and children's rights in Afghanistan under the Taliban. She visited the United States in February 2005 and presented at the Peace Prize Forum at Augsburg College in Minneapolis where thousands heard first-hand the incredible story of Afghanistan under the Taliban's brutality. Today, Afghanistan is on the path searching for democracy, stability, hope for freedom, better opportunities, and fairness for all with the help of compassionate people inside and outside of the country.

To the west of Afghanistan lies another country that violates human rights and places no value on women. A report from a human rights organization asserts that a woman in Iran "was lashed fifty times for being present at a family gathering where men other than her father and brother were present."

Women in oppressed countries such as Iran and Afghanistan are under so much pressure and know no way to defend themselves. Iraq is not excluded from this realm of tyranny. While Saddam Hussein was in power, woman in Iraq were deprived of social rights. They experienced domestic repression and aggressive militant assaults throughout the country.

According to the Iraq Foundation, an advocate for democracy and human rights in Iraq, operating as a non-profit organization in the United States, the militia created by Uday Saddam's oldest son in 1994, were engaged in beheading women who were caught in immoral conduct that were completely contradicting Islamic laws. "The militia, which acted independently of the military establishment, had reportedly sought out women suspected of prostitution and men suspected of procurement, and summarily carried out street executions in several areas of Baghdad."

The Iraq Foundation reports that "The beheadings, which lacked any form of judicial process, were reportedly carried out by sword in front of the suspects' houses, in view of their families, members of the Ba'th Party and women's organizations." It should be noted that Uday was killed by U.S. forces during a failing resistance during Iraq war.

A recently published book, *Honor Lost: Love and Death in Modern-Day Jordan* by Norma Khouri, details the ancient tradition that encourages the murder of women considered to have dishonored their families in the country of Jordan. This book chronicles the life and death of the author's best friend (Dalia) who was killed by her own father — who stabbed her 12 times in the chest and received a three month sentence from the religious court in Jordan. That's because Dalia's death was — quote — an "honor killing" — meant to cleanse the family's honor because Dalia, who was 25 years-old and unmarried, had a boyfriend.

Women in Saudi Arabia and other neighboring countries are not given any rights to be independent and make their own decisions. African countries also have a long history of violating human rights.

Amina Lawal, a 31-year-old Muslim woman, was sentenced to death by stoning by a Sharia [Islamic] court at Bakori in Katsina State in northern Nigeria. Amina allegedly confessed to having had a child while divorced. Pregnancy outside of marriage is sufficient evidence for a woman to be convicted of adultery according to this new law for Muslims, introduced in the northern states of Nigeria.

Amnesty International provides up-to-date information on the violation of human rights around the world. Officials there said the most effective way to put a stop to Amina's horrifying sentence was to e-mail the Nigerian Ambassador to the United States.

An Update on Amina's Story

Over 1.2 million people sent e-mails to help! And it made a difference—while the law has not officially changed, the Nigerian government has publicly announced that they will not enforce any stoning sentences handed down by the religious court.

Women in the Western World

Women in the western world do not experience formidable manipulation or death by their governments. Nevertheless, they are struggling for equal opportunity for employment, the elimination of discrimination, and the abolishment of rape, battering, sexual harassment, sexual assault, and bigotry. In the United States, women have made remarkable achievements on women's rights. There are thousands of women's organizations in the United States, some are national, and most are available in each state. In Minnesota alone, for example, there are 346 organizations that advocate women's rights in all aspects of life. The global list of women's organizations and the list of all women's organizations in the U.S. that is sorted by their zip codes can be obtained from www.google.com or any other search engine.

As a random selection it should be noted that organizations such as NOW (National Organization for Women), National Association for Female Executives, American Business Women's Association, and Association of Women in Communications, are among thousands of organizations in the U.S. that nationally and internationally advocate women's rights. Another organization that is worth mentioning is the Women's Alliance which provides professional attire, career skills training, and related services to low-income women seeking employment. Famous individuals such as Coretta Scott King (widow of Dr. Martin Luther King), Rosalyn Carter (wife of president Jimmy Carter), Senator Hillary Clinton, Shrin Ebadi (2003 Noble Peace Prize laureate), Dr. Sima Samar, (human rights advocate from Afghanistan and 2001 John Humphrey Freedom Award Recipient), Maya Angelou, Oprah Winfrey, Barbara Walters, Star Jones Reynolds, and Lucy Liu, are a short list of great human beings who are strong voices of women not only in the United States, but around the world as well. Young women are encouraged to join at least one organization of their choice and keep the legacy of women's rights strong and steady to benefit all women in America and around the world.

Human Rights in the United States

In 1776 when our founding fathers structured the democracy in this country they were optimistic that people from all backgrounds could live together in peace and harmony. Although the civil war and other historic events such as the civil rights movement proved otherwise, we built a society that is a role model for other countries around the world. Almost every state in the union has a human rights commission and the efforts to establish a human rights commission in each American city is commendable. The League of Human Rights Commissions in each state provide educational support to human rights activists who voluntarily spend their time to protect the rights of people from all different races and ethnicities.

Despite the efforts of humanitarian organizations that represent the American people, occasionally, the U.S. government does not represent its people when it comes to Human Rights. More than 40 million people in the United States suffer from poverty and homelessness (Mittal & Rosset, 1999). Therefore, as long as we witness hunger and homelessness in America it is ironic to carry the torch of human rights in the world. The Statue of Liberty in New York is the symbol representing a country which promotes democracy, freedom and human rights for all. We need to have strong voices in Congress to rejuvenate policies for a better America. We need to talk about "peace" not "war." All human rights must be protected at home before we become advocates and promoters of human rights around the world.

Human Rights Commissions across the United States

From the genesis of humanity up to the present, the issue of human rights has been the focal point of civilization for the reason that the rights of humans are violated by those who choose to influence power and supremacy over others. In the course of history, poets, writers, and speakers have given awareness messages and declarations to enunciate that human rights should be protected. Likewise, for the well-being of citizens in Chaska, a diverse suburb, we put together a commission that ensures all are treated equally with common interests-with no difference to what Adam Smith said many years ago: "It is usually by pursuing our interests with due consideration to the interest of others that we contribute most to the common well-being."

The following quote from the by-laws of the Chaska Human Rights Commission—a small quality town in Minnesota—specifies the purpose and the mission of their Commission:

> The purpose of the Commission is to secure for all citizens, through education and prevention, equal opportunities for employment, housing, public information, public services, education, fair treatment, and full participation in affairs of the community. The Commission's mission is to proactively partner with government, business, educators, religious, service and other organizations to promote a community of harmony and respect for the rights and dignity of all.

In simpler terms, the focus of the Chaska Human Rights Commission revolves around community values, human connections, and above all, human dignity. The Mayor of this small town shows a great compassion for community values: "It is very important that we always revolve our discussions around the community values that speak directly toward Human Rights issues." The Commission which consists of nine volunteer members is putting all its time and efforts to be a useful and effective entity for Chaska and other neighboring localities.

In order to accomplish the mission specified in the by-laws, the activities of the Human Rights Commission shall focus on the following areas: 1) Educating the community on the issues of discrimination and cultural diversity, and 2) Periodically assessing the extent to which the human rights of the citizens of Chaska are adequately and satisfactorily protected and recommending necessary action(s).

The commission will continue to serve the community and would like to communicate with all citizens. A small U.S. town such as Chaska by having a human rights commission deserves the praise of democracy and the admiration of human rights activists.

Human Rights after September 11, 2001

Unfortunately, human rights are not protected in many countries around the world. In a clearer sense, there are no human rights in those countries. Some of the Middle Eastern countries have been observed by Amnesty International and the facts are devastating. Prisoners are tortured in many inhumane ways, children are molested, women and young girls are raped in front of their families. This corruptive mentality of those who form the ruling authorities of such countries not only devastated their own nations, but has become a criminal commodity for exporting to the western world and especially America. We are fortunate to live in a democratic society where human rights are protected and respected. We need to show to some parts of the world that human lives are valuable and living in a free society coincides with the respect and protection of human dignity.

On June 2, 2003, it was reported that human rights violations have been documented by the Department of Justice's internal investigation of its treatment of non-citizens detained after September 11. The hard-hitting 198-page report released by the Office of the Inspector General (OIG), an internal agency watchdog, confirms abuses reported by Human Rights Watch, including prolonged detention without charge, denial of access to legal counsel, and excessively harsh conditions of confinement. (Human Rights Watch, 2003) Wendy Patten, the U.S. advocacy director at Human Rights Watch believes that "the report is a superb expose of how the Justice Department circumvented people's basic rights after September 11."

In the wake of the September 11th attacks, the Justice Department detained over 1,200 non-citizens, primarily from Middle Eastern, South Asian, and North African countries. The government used immigration charges as a pretext to detain 766 non-citizens while it investigated possible links to terrorism. At most, no more than a handful of these "special interest" detainees have been charged with a terrorism-related crime. According to Human Rights Watch, the

Justice Department has refused to release the identities of these detainees and has conducted the majority of their immigration hearings in secret (Human Rights Watch, 2003).

In May 2005, it was reported by *Newsweek* that in Gunatánamo Bay, Cuba where foreign detainees are in captivity, the Koran, the holy book of Muslims had been desecrated by a U.S. interrogator. The Koran was flushed down a toilet. A week later after some Islamic nations flooded the streets and violently protested against the United States, leaving 16 people dead, the *Newsweek* apologized for reporting it wrong! (Kurtz, 2005) Almost all major news agencies were on the same page by reporting that "FBI memo reports Guantánamo Bay guards flushing the Koran" (Malkin, 2005). The desecration of the Koran created anger and animosity towards Americans in the Islamic world. The United States government is liable for any action that Armed Forces personnel and civilian authority commit either at home or abroad. The nature of the Guantánamo Bay incident is under investigation to identify who did what under what circumstances, yet it damaged U.S. credibility tremendously in most parts of the world and many people around the world viewed it as a human rights violation.

Does the United States Need Human Rights Education?

Not long ago (1997), in a national survey, Human Rights USA, a partnership for human rights education, examined the levels of knowledge and attitude of Americans on human rights. The results of this survey were astonishing! Only 8% of adults and 4% of young people knew about the Universal Declaration of Human Rights (UDHR). Although on a daily basis we hear from news agencies and watch major media in the USA about the crises of human rights, still 90% of the population is oblivious when it comes to issues of human rights (Flowers, et al., 2000). The survey revealed the following:

- 83% believed that the USA is not fully in compliance of the UDHR
- 63% believed that the poor in the USA are constantly discriminated against
- 61% believed that the disabled in the USA are constantly discriminated against
- 54% believed that the elderly in the USA are constantly discriminated against

- 61% believed that gays and lesbians in the USA are constantly discriminated against
- 50% believed that Native Americans in the USA are constantly discriminated against
- 41% believed that African Americans in the USA are constantly discriminated against (Flowers, et al., 2000)

The outcome of the above mentioned survey discloses that indeed we need to have human rights education in our local communities, in our schools, and in our institutions of higher education.

Summary

It's been more than half a century since the Universal Declaration of Human Rights (UDHR) came in to existence. Yet, almost half of the world (97 countries) arguably lack or violate human rights. The devastation of poverty and homelessness around the world, even in rich and industrial countries, make human relations and global interactions difficult, sometimes, impossible. The violation of human rights in many parts of the world, particularly the rights of children and women, receive little or no attention from the international community despite the sanctity of the Universal Declaration of Human Rights. Amid all the problems human beings have to tackle with, terrorism adds a new chapter to the challenge of human rights and cultural diversity.

Test Your Knowledge

Part One: Identify true or false statements

Instruction: In front of each statement below put "T" for a true statement, and "F" for a false statement.

1.____Hunger and homelessness are the two issues that need the most human rights attention in the U.S.

2.____ Women in the U.S. are still the victims of sexual assaults, battering, discrimination and terrible domestic crimes.

3.____ Amnesty International provides financial assistance and legal services on the violation of human rights around the world.

4.____ In most parts of the western world human rights were violated in the name of national security after 9/11.

5.____ America did not invent human rights.

6.____Universal Declaration of Human Rights consists of 20 articles.

7.____Elenor and Franklin Roosevelt wrote the Universal Declaration of Human Rights.

8.____Human rights are violated in more than 60 percent of the world's nations.

9.____The most famous example of natural rights is the "Declaration of Independence" asserted by Thomas Jefferson.

10.____The majority of Arab immigrants live in Cleveland.

Part Two: Discussion Questions

1. Why do so many countries in the world lack human rights?
2. How does terrorism violate human rights?
3. Which basic human rights are important to you? And why?
4. What is the reason the United States government does not prioritize human rights in its agenda?
5. How could we protect our national security without damaging and defaming others with different national origins?
6. Using Guantánamo Bay as an example: is it acceptable to protect our human rights and violate others'?
7. Why not create a department of "peace" rather than "war" if we believe in democracy at home and around the world?
8. Does the policy of "at will" violate human rights in employment?

"I hold it to be the inalienable right of anybody to go to hell in his own way."

-Robert Frost
American Poet

"Be as beneficent as the sun or the sea, but if your rights as a rational being are trenched on, die on the first inch of your territory."

-Ralph Waldo Emerson
American essayist, poet, and philosopher

"Today's human rights violations are the causes of tomorrow's conflicts."

-Mary Robinson
U.N. High Commissioner for Human Rights

Chapter 10: Globalization and the Future of Diversity

"It has been said that arguing against globalization is like arguing against the laws of gravity."

-*Kofi Annan*, UN Secretary General

"Globalization is not a phenomenon. It is not just some passing trend. Today it is an overarching international system shaping the domestic politics and foreign relations of virtually every country, and we need to understand it as such.

Thomas Friedman, The New York Columnist

Objectives

- Define globalization
- Identify the many faces of globalization
- Explore the use of globalization in a multicultural society
- Demystify the incorrect sentiments about globalization
- Analyze the impact of globalization on cultural diversity
- Elucidate the future of diversity in the contemporary world

Introduction

Globalization has been a controversial subject for many years. It depends where you are on the planet earth, what political or economical philosophy you follow, and how it may affect your future, then you define it accordingly. To globalize something simply means to make it available and accessible for everyone in the world. When McDonald's franchise system expanded its wings beyond the U.S. borders it opened many branches around the world. In 1995 there were 62 McDonald's in China, in 2000 the number jumped to 326. Today (August, 2005), McDonald's has about 600 stores in China and is looking to have 1000 by the year 2006. (Chinadaily.com, 2005) McDonald's has been expanding its operations in Europe and other Asian countries as well. In 2001, there was a report that McDonald's operates about 28000 restaurants in over 100 countries (Middleton, 2003). There are 6000 McDonald's in Europe (Chinadaily.com, 2005).

Coca Cola, Pepsi, Levi's Jeans, T.G.I. Friday's and other corporations as such are other examples of globalization efforts that are directly associated with economic expansions generated from the United States. Now, globalization refers to many things from many parts of the world. Today, besides the economy, other systems of culture such as religion, politics, family values, and education are marketable subjects of globalization. For example, Islamic fundamentalists try to globalize their religion, Christian Evangelists would like to globalize Christianity (as they have been doing for decades), playing soccer is becoming globally accepted, and the Internet has opened a new frontier in global communication. Interestingly enough, e-Bay has more than 168 million customers in 33 countries to this date. Globalization received much publicity in recent years and will continue to be a hot issue for the rest of the 21st century. Cultural diversity and globalization are related through intercultural communication, commonalities, and differences. As we get closer to a more diverse future, globalization becomes an ongoing matter of discussion all over the globe. There are arguments about the advantages and disadvantages which globalization offers each society. This chapter explores some of the positive and negative attributes of globalization.

What is "globalization"?

Simply, globalization refers to goods and services that are available on a global scale. For example, most countries, particularly, in Europe, Asia, and Latin America adopted the American cowboy blue jeans. They look good, last long, are comfortable, and are reasonable (with the exception of black markets in closed economies). People in communist China like to eat McDonald's hamburgers, listen to American rap music, and drink Coca Cola. The same situation can be observed in many other countries such as Japan, Taiwan, and South Korea. Globalization is the result of peoples' ability to create large economic systems that involve worldwide banking, open trade markets, and the culture of effective communication.

Globalization builds positive bridges between continents and regions of the world. For many years we looked at Communist China as an unfriendly giant with nothing in common with the western world.

As a result of globalization, today China welcomes Americans for business and leisure, shares its cultural values with the rest of the world, and has opened an economic relationship with the European community and other regions of the world.

While explaining diversity, globalization, and public policy in Canada, Abu-Laban & Gabriel (2002) believe that: "...the technological and cultural flows associated with globalization serve to connect peoples and countries around the world; moreover, events and activities in one part of the world can have consequences for individuals and communities in distant parts." (p. 17)

Globalization has many defendants and some opponents even in capitalist societies such as America. For many years, it was known as a phenomenon that started from the capitalist countries, namely the U.S., Canada, and the western European nations. In defense of globalization many prominent individuals such as Thomas Friedman, the *New York Times* columnist; Jagdish Bhagwati, a professor at Columbia University and one of the world's foremost authorities on international trade; Peter Berger, a sociology professor at Boston University have emphasized the inevitability of globalization. Thomas Friedman defines globalization with the following words (Walsh, 2005):

> Globalization can be incredibly empowering and incredibly coercive. It can democratize opportunity and democratize panic. It makes the whales bigger and the minnows stronger. It leaves you behind faster and faster, and it catches up to you faster and faster. While it is homogenizing cultures, it is also enabling people to share their unique individuality farther and wider.

There's no way to ignore or devalue globalization. Our interconnectedness globally in recent years has proven that globalization brings more benefits than harmful damages. Of course, we should bear in mind that any intention of exploitation of natural and human resources in poor countries for the sake of people in rich countries should not be tolerated. The motto "Think Globally, Act Locally" has given encouragement to millions of people on the planet. It is an excellent message that works in many areas, from human rights to environmental protection, to social relationships and human communications.

The act of terrorism is an inhumane undertaking that unfortunately has become globalized. If in most cases globalization has provided unity and closer relationships among nations, other faces of globalization have generated negative thoughts among people in rich and poor countries. In case a super power decides to invade a country in the name of liberation, peace, democracy, and impose its way of life upon that victimized country, that kind of globalization is not welcomed in the world.

The Many Faces of Globalization

Globalization has many forms. The most important kind of globalization that affects the majority of the world population is economic globalization which has created anti-globalization as well. International trade organizations, such as the World Trade Organization (WTO), the World Bank, the International Monetary Fund (IMF), the North American Free Trade Agreement (NAFTA), and many other financial organizations that are involved in international business are the architects of economic globalization. "These institutions have often been targeted at their annual meetings by demonstrators who object to their 'conditionalities' for assistance or their ambition to liberalize trade, depending on the institution being attacked" (Bhagwati, 2004).

Cultural globalization is another form of globalization which has received academic attention in recent years. From America to Africa and from the Mediterranean to Southeast Asia, cultural globalization has been the subject of discussion among many sociologists. Cultural globalization is seen as "emissions" of cultural methods from nation to nation, or from one region to another. Peter Berger believes that "cultural globalization is the movement of goods and ideas (cultural freight) from the West to the rest of the world (Srinivas, 2002), but it is also possible that cultural globalization operates in a non-western fashion as well. Today, Islamic fundamentalists are promoting their religion to the rest of the world, and cultural models of the East such as meditation, yoga, spiritual healing, massage, and acupuncture therapy are being practiced in the West. For many years, the western way of life, social norms, and characteristics of western cultures have been emitted to other parts of the world. Economic prosperity in corporate America, for example, has tempted other nations to make a change in their socio-economic styles and follow the American way of life. In recent years, more than ever, communication technologies have evolved for the sake of cultural globalization. The Internet since the early 1990s has made a great evolution in many phases that we seem to be living in a "flat world" as stated by the prominent author Thomas Friedman.

Cultural globalization is welcomed in many societies as long as religious and traditional beliefs are not damaged by it. A good example was preached by, the late Ayatollah Khomeini, the Leader of the Islamic Revolution of Iran. He repeatedly asserted that not everything from the West is bad. His famous line translated in this manner: "As to your best interests acquire their [the West] best technology and education and throw away things that facilitate corruption, and immorality, [namely fashion, Hollywood, and related matters]."

Indeed, the western world can enjoy and benefit from the rich culture and civilizations around the world. The West, including the North American continent, have long been enjoying the cultures and traditions (food, artifacts, etc.) of the Greeks, Egyptians, Persians, Indians, Chinese, and Japanese, to name a few.

Cultural globalization is not a new phenomenon. Western civilization with all its attributes was adopted by Turkish people more than 70 years ago when their leader Kemal Atatürk made a drastic change in many phases of the socio-economic system of Turkey. Their writing style was changed to Latin, women were free to follow European fashions, and modernity was brought to the major cities, especially the greater metropolitan area of Istanbul. Opponents of western modernity have been confronting this life style for many decades and in some ways have acquired their desires by establishing Islamic schools, enforcing the wearing of the hijab (the covering of hair and bodies of women), and incurring activity in the political spectrum.

In describing cultural globalization in Turkey, Ozbudun & Keyman (2002) assert that "cultural globalization creates both the universalization of Western values and cultural patterns and at the same time the revitalization of local values and traditions." (p. 301) By "the revitalization of local values and traditions," they mean the resurgence of Islam in terms of alternative modernity. Ozbudun and Keyman do not condemn cultural globalization by mentioning the resurgence of Islam, rather they are trying to keep both sides happy, the western world, and the Islamic insurgents who were given credit for bringing another form of modernity to the country, namely "the resurgence of Islam." This new argument may not be supported by many in the neighboring country of Iran, who witnessed that the Islamic revolution not only demolished Western values and cultural patterns in Iran, the resurgence of Islam was not seen as an alternative modernity but a required way of life.

As mentioned before, cultural globalization may not be seen as an agent of modernity and progress in some countries. The controlling factor is fundamental beliefs in traditions and remarkably the religions that people strongly follow, especially in Islamic countries. Nevertheless, many Islamic societies have welcomed Western values and cultural patterns while at the same time value their own. Among these countries, are the Persian Gulf states (United Arab Emirates), Kuwait, Bahrain, Qatar, Morocco, Lebanon, Jordan, and Malaysia.

The Taiwanese have enjoyed the impact of cultural globalization simply because they are open, plural, with the ever changing attitudes and self adaptation which make the nation a modern society (Hsiao, 2002).

In China, cultural globalization demonstrates a new form that is not universally applicable. In other words, it is a process that is managed by the government, while the elite and the populace proactively team up to welcome the emerging global culture and claim the ownership of the new paradigm (Yan, 2002).

Globalization will soon reach all societies despite opposing viewpoints in some countries. One day, hopefully soon, the closed economy nations such as Cuba whose people are suffering from repression and dictatorship will see the light of globalization at the end of the dark tunnel. Unfortunately, Cuba, due to present circumstances, has not shown the openness necessary to adjust itself to the growing trend other nations have seen as a result of globalization. Cubans are desperate to see the effects of globalization on their society.

Anti-globalization

Those who oppose globalization strongly argue that globalization is an instrument of poverty and exploitation of the weak by the strong nations. Anti-globalization, therefore, is in line with imperialism and capitalism. It is interesting to note that anti-globalization is more prevalent in rich countries than poor ones.

Opponents to free trade and the ways it is handled by some international institutions such as the World Trade Organization (as argued by some agitated groups) do not consider globalization as good business!

In 1999 a violent demonstration broke up the ministerial meeting of the WTO in Seattle, Washington. The demonstrators demanded the immediate cancellation of the meeting for many reasons including the WTO's harmful and inhumane policies on using natural resources, the environmental degradation of human activity and so forth.

Anti-corporation, anti-multinationals, anti-global economies, anti-capitalism, and therefore anti-globalization are all negative manifestations of progress, development, and modernization. Another source of anti-globalization is the anti-Americanism that is growing these days. The military power, invasion, liberation, occupation, and presence of American troops around the world and the economic hegemony of the Unites States have created bad sentiments in many parts of the world, jealousy in competitor-nations and animosity in developing or poor countries. One of the most notorious anti-American organizations is Osama bin-Ladin's Alqaeda terrorist organization whose 9/11 attacks on the U.S. soil devastated many lives of the world's citizens, thus had a huge effect on cultural diversity in North America and other parts of the world. Osama is belligerently opposed to modernization, cultural globalization, international relations, and social change in any form or method. He does not necessarily condemn capitalism, because he and his family are the richest people in Saudi Arabia! Anti-globalization sentiments in poorer countries may be associated with social predicaments and/or frenzied economies.

After all, it is up to the political regime in each country to promote, condemn, or to be oblivious to globalization. Governments can remove obstacles in favor of flow of the trade and global investments. Latin American countries have been dealing with globalization for decades. The United States of America, Canada, and some European countries have had long histories of dealing with South America, Asia, Africa, and the Middle East for the objective of global investment and trade. In this respect, those countries with good relationships with the Western World have had better opportunities to revitalize their economy. Conversely, the nations with internal problems, disordered economies, and some history of animosity with the U.S. and major European countries have been reluctant to perpetuate globalization; thus have remained idle with no significant progress in socio-economic conditions.

How Can Globalization Help Diversity?

Globalization has been the subject of many books in recent years. Therefore, it is not easy to talk about globalization in a few pages. So far, we have learned how globalization, especially in the age of rapid communication systems and the prosperity of the world economy can bring people together and has become an agent of change for millions around the world.

Cultural diversity in America (the U.S., Canada, Mexico, and Latin America) is growing incredibly due to the interconnectedness and accessibility to human resources. Since 1985, more than ever, we have witnessed more human relationships not only within a culture but among many cultures and civilizations in the world. Simon (2001) expresses his understanding of globalization in this manner: "globalization has offered new challenges to manage our minds, words, and actions amid the shifting relationships, the stresses and strains that arise between the world's nations, cultures, and regions" (p. 91).

Globalization, with its many shapes and forms, has changed the philosophical attitudes of many nations. For years, the former Soviet Union (now Russia), China, and other satellites of them were reluctant to open their doors to the rest of the world, specifically to the capitalist countries. Today, due to globalization, people from diverse cultural backgrounds have the opportunity to electronically connect with the people of these nations or for educational or economic adventures make a trip and explore their differences.

The United States has a great impact on promoting globalization in the world. Who could imagine that as a result of the Internet, a couple can establish an Internet auction company (e-Bay) which in 2005 could operate in 33 countries and give services to 168 million customers? This largest on-line auction company in the world has made economic and cultural globalization possible on a daily basis. It has embraced people from all different backgrounds while improving their socio-economic conditions.

The 21st century is the century of diversity. As positive globalization connects people from all parts of the world, the interaction among people becomes easier with less prejudicial and ethnocentric attitudes. There is no doubt that many nations open their hearts and minds to people from different backgrounds. Good Samaritans from the Western world help millions of people around the world who are very poor, hungry, ill, or on the verge of death. An excellent example of this humanitarian effort is Live 8 whose mission is to make poverty history. Livetechnorati.com (2005) provides more detail on Live 8.

> Live 8 is a series of concerts and events across the world which are being staged to highlight the problem of global poverty. It's a chance for ordinary people to call on world leaders at this year's G8 summit and tell them to put a stop to the needless deaths of 30,000 children every single day. On [July 6th] 2005, the leaders of Great Britain, the USA, Canada, France, Germany, Italy, Japan and Russia will meet at Gleneagles in Scotland to talk about world affairs, including Africa. They will be presented with a workable plan to double aid, drop the debt and make trade laws fair. The G8 summit is our opportunity to demand that the world's most influential leaders take action now. Live 8 has organized concerts in Philadelphia, Berlin, London, Rome, Paris and Edinburgh, with 100 artists, a million spectators, two billion viewers and one message: Make Poverty History.

Bob Geldof, the organizer of Live 8 urges people around the world, especially in the rich nations to help Africa get out of poverty. They don't need just our money, they need our voices too!

"The future is about 'diversity' not about money, oil, cars, and so on," says a young Native American entrepreneur from Canada who is in the communication/advertising business. It is important to spread the message around the world as the slogan of diversitypromotions.com asserts: "embrace diversity, embrace our world."

Summary

Globalization is perceived as goods and services accessible to people around the world. Globalization has been a controversial subject due to the fact that it has economic advantages to many actors in the western world and those who promote it in certain areas of the globe. There are pros and cons when the subject of globalization is for discussion. Many believe that globalization brings socio-economic advantages, especially creating jobs for millions of people around the world. Those who are anti-globalization condemn the activities that they believe are associated with discrimination, environmental exploitation, violation of human rights, and breach of international law such as child labor, sweat shops, and abuse of people in the globalized countries for the sake of globalization activities.

Globalization, despite of controversial justifications is a conduit for human interactions around the world. Particularly, in recent years we have witnessed the global communication has immeasurably progressed due to invention of the Internet. People from different cultures and traditions interact globally in order to satisfy their needs locally. In the 21st century, the progress of human intelligence will continue to facilitate more globalization thus a more accessible advantages for survival and even prosperity in many phases of human life. Cultural diversity will benefit from globalization because people know more about their differences and the ways to reconcile them for better living and working environments.

Test Your Knowledge

Part One: Survey

Instructions: Next to each statement place the number that is most suitable to your understanding of this chapter.
1 = strongly agree   2 = agree   3 = neutral   4 = disagree   5 = strongly disagree

1._____ To globalize something simply means to make it available and accessible for everyone in the world.

2._____ Besides the economy, other systems of culture such as religion, politics, family values, and education are marketable subjects of globalization.

3._____ The way free trade is handled by some international institutions such as the World Trade Organization does not represent good business.

4._____ Globalization, with its many shapes and forms, has changed the philosophical attitudes of many nations.

5._____ Cultural globalization may not be seen as an agent of modernity and progress in some countries.

6._____ If a super power decides to invade a country in the name of liberation, peace, democracy, and impose its way of life upon that victimized country, that kind of globalization is not welcomed in the world.

7._____ "Globalization has offered new challenges to manage our minds, words, and actions amid the shifting relationships, the stresses and strains that arise between the world's nations, cultures, and regions."

8._____ Today, cyberspace has created a great contribution to cultural globalization. People from diverse cultural backgrounds have the opportunity to electronically connect with the people of these nations or for educational or economic adventures make a trip and explore their differences.

9._____ Economic prosperity in corporate America has tempted other nations to make a change in their socio-economic styles and follow the American way of life.

10._____A person in China does not see globalization the same way as a person sees it in the Middle East.

Part Two: Discussion questions

1. What should the WTO and other gigantic financial institutions do to satisfy their opponents?
2. To what extent should globalization be promoted?
3. Why are some people in rich and poor nations against globalization?
4. How do you define terrorism as being a threat to globalization?
5. What is the correlation between a cultural attaché in each embassy around the world and the concept of cultural globalization?
6. What should the United States do to improve its relationships with trouble-making countries such as Iran and North Korea? Should we approach them for a positive globalization?

"It has been said that arguing about globalization is like arguing against the laws of gravity."

-Kofi Annan
U.N. Secretary General

"We must take care that globalization does not become something people become afraid of."
-Gerhard Schroede
German Chancellor

"Globalization is not something we can hold off or turn off...it is the economic equivalent of a force of nature—like wind or water."
-President Bill Clinton

Glossary

Acculturation. Cultural modification of an individual, group, or people by adapting to or borrowing traits from another culture; a merging of cultures as a result of prolonged contact.

Advantaged. Being in a relatively favored position.

Affirmative –action. Action taken to provide equal opportunity for women and minorities and other protected classes.

Afro-centrism. Centered on Africa and things peculiar to Africa.

African American. (1) Refers to Black individuals living in the United States with African ancestry; (2) Refers to individuals of African heritage living in the United States having similar experiences, culture heritage and ancestry of former slaves.

Ageism. Discrimination of individuals based on their age, i.e. of the elderly based on the notion that they are incapable of performing certain functions such as driving, or of the young based on the notion that they are immature and therefore incapable of performing certain tasks.

Alaska Native. A person having origins in any of the original peoples of North America or who maintains cultural identification through tribal affiliation or community recognition.

Anti-Semitism. Hatred toward Jews; prejudicial belief in the "racial" or religious inferiority of Jews. The term itself was first used in 1879.

Asian. A person having origins in any of the original peoples of the Far East, Southeast Asia, the Indian Subcontinent, or the Pacific Islands. This includes people from China, Japan, Korea, the Philippine Islands, American Samoa, India and Vietnam.

Asian American. Refers to individuals living in the United States with Asian ancestry.

Assimilation. The process whereby a minority group gradually adopts the customs and attitudes of the majority.

Bisexual. Individuals attracted to members of the male and female sex.

Bigotry. The attitude of intolerance toward anything not of one's own group.

Black, non-Hispanic. A person having origins in any of the Black racial groups of Africa (except those of Hispanic origin).

Caucasian. Of, relating to, or being a racial classification traditionally distinguished by very light to brown skin pigmentation and straight to wavy or curly hair and including peoples indigenous to Europe, northern Africa, the Middle East, western Asia, and India.

Chicana. A female American of Mexican descent

Chicano. A male American of Mexican descent

Civil Rights Legislation. Laws prohibiting discrimination for reasons of race, gender, ethnicity, etc.

Class. Category of division based on economic status; members of a class are theoretically assumed to possess similar cultural, political and economic characteristics and principles.

Classism. Discrimination based on class.

Conflict. A state of disharmony between incompatible or antithetical persons, ideas, or interests; a clash.

Cultural heritage. Characteristics, traditions and birthright of a community passed down through generations of people.

Diaspora. (1881) the settling of scattered colonies of Jews outside Palestine after the Babylonian exile. A historical dispersion of a group of people deriving from similar origins, i.e. the African Diaspora includes African Americans, Africans, Caribbeans, Afro-Russians, Black Brazilians, Afro-Latinos etc...

Difference. The quality of being dissimilar; a disagreement or controversy.

Disadvantaged. (1) A historically oppressed group having less than sufficient resources to fund all of basic needs; without expendable income; (2) A group characterized by disproportionate economic, social, and political disadvantages.

Discrimination. A biased decision based on a prejudice against an individual or a group characterized by race, class, sexual orientation, age, disabilities, etc.

Diversity. The quality of being different; a situation that includes representation of all groups within a prescribed environment, such as a university or a workplace. This term most commonly refers to differences between cultural or social groups—which entails religion, sexual orientation, political affiliation, etc. An emphasis on accepting and respecting cultural differences by recognizing that no one culture is intrinsically superior to another underlies the current usage of the term.

Diversity training. A course that teaches awareness of racial, ethnic, and gender differences among people and issues caused by those differences.

Emigrant. One who leaves his/her country of origin to reside in a foreign country.

Enculturation. Learning about your own culture

Ethnic double consciousness. Facing discrimination from two standpoints, e.g. minority women who face both racial and gender discrimination.

Ethnicity. A quality assigned to a specific group of people historically connected by a common national origin or language. Ethnic classification is used for identification rather than differentiation.

Ethnocentrism. A practice of unconsciously or consciously privileging a certain ethnic group over others. This involves judging other groups by the values of one's own group.

Etiquette. The practices and forms prescribed by social convention or by authority.

Eurocentrism. The practice of consciously or unconsciously privileging the culture of Europe over other cultures.

European American. An individual living in the United States with European ancestry.

Exclusion. Leaving out certain people or denying their rights and privileges.

Expatriate. A person who leaves his or her native country to live and work elsewhere. Expatriation is often a temporary assignment by one's organization for a specific job abroad.

Federal Glass Ceiling Commission. An organization within the Department of Labor that deals with the restricted upward movement for women in organization.

Feminism. Movement advocating equal rights, status, ability, and treatment of women, based on the belief that women are not in any way inferior to men.

Gender. System of sexual classification based on the social construction of the categories "men" and "women," as opposed to sex which is based on biological and physical differences which form the categories "male" and "female."

Glass ceiling. A term for the maximum position and salary some claim minorities and women are allowed to reach without any chances of further promotion or advancement within an employment scenario.

Globalization. Globalization is the result of peoples' ability to create large economic systems which involve worldwide banking, open trade markets, and the culture of effective communication.

Heterosexism. Social structures and practices which serve to elevate and enforce heterosexuality while subordinating or suppressing other forms of sexuality.

Heterosexual. Pertaining to individuals attracted to the opposite sex.

Hispanic. A person of Mexican, Puerto Rican, Cuban, Central or South America, or other Spanish culture or origin, regardless of race.

Hispanic American. Individuals living in the United States with ancestry from Hispanic, that is Spanish-speaking countries.

Homosexual. Individuals attracted to members of one's own sex.

Hostile work environment. A work culture marked by negativism and antagonism toward some groups.

Human interactions. Communication and other contact and actions between people.

Human relationships. Attitude or stance that people assume toward one another. Connections and dealings among people.

Immigrant. A person who resides in a nation, country, or region other than that of his/her origin. Also known as non-native, outlander, outsider, alien, etc.

Indigenous. Originating from a culture with ancient ties to the land in which a group resides.

Inter-racial. Involving more than one race.

Intra-gender. Within the same gender.

Intra-racial. Within the same race.

Invisible differences. Differences between people that are not immediately apparent or obvious.

Jew(s). Members of a people based on a background of shared historical experience and of religious heritage (Judaism). Membership is through birth or conversion. Not all Jews are religious. Most North American Jews are descended from immigrants from Eastern Europe. Jews can be understood in both ethnic and religious terms.

Kwanzaa. (meaning "the first fruit") is a seven-day cultural celebration of African Americans (December 26 through January 1) began by Dr. Maulana Karenga in 1966.

Latina. female native or inhabitant of Latin America; a female of Latin American origin living in the U.S.

Latino. A male native or inhabitant of Latin America; a male of Latin American origin living in the U.S.

Managing diversity. A managerial process that creates an environment that is non-hostile for all employees and in which all employees are able to contribute to their fullest.

Media. Conveyer of data to the public through newspapers, magazines, Television, Radio, Internet, etc., and reaching a large audience.

Mentor. A high ranking person, an influential organization member, an instructor, a manager, or a supervisor who is committed to providing career support to an individual.

Minority. Term used to describe a member of a group or a group that represents a relatively smaller percentage of the overall population of a nation/state/ continent, etc.

Multiculturalism. The practice of acknowledging and respecting the various cultures, religions, races, ethnicities, attitudes and opinions within an environment.

National origin. System of classification based on nation from which a person originates, regardless of the nation in which he/she currently resides.

Native American. A person having origins in any of the original peoples of North America or who maintains cultural identification through tribal affiliation or community recognition.

Organizational culture. A work environment created by an organization's principles, norms, policies, practices, and relationships between people.

Oriental. Relating to or deriving from the language, traditions, or cultures of the peoples of Asian nations in the region designated as "the Orient," or "the East," by Europeans. This term is conspicuously eurocentric as "the East" is constructed as being opposed to a fixed reference point, "the West," or western Europe.

Overt discrimination. Open and observable prejudicial actions or behavior.

Pan-Africanism. (1) Describes the theory relating to the desire to educate all peoples of the African diaspora of their common plight and of the connections between them, e.g. a problem faced by one group affects the lives of other groups as well; (2) Theory relating to the desire to link all African countries across the continent through a common government, language, ideology, or belief.

People of color. A term used to describe all non-white racial or ethnic groups.

Polarization. A divisive concentration of conflicting or contrasting positions.

Prejudge. Judging beforehand without adequate evidence.

Prejudice. A preconceived preference or idea; bias; adverse judgment without examining the facts; exerting bias and bigotry based on uniformed stereotypes.

Prejudice-free work environment. A work climate in which no one is treated with prejudice; a non-hostile environment.

Principle. A code of conduct that influences how people think and act.

Privilege. Power and advantages benefiting a group derived from the historical oppression and exploitation of other groups.

Privileged. Having special permission, advantages, or rights.

Quota. An allotment or proportional share assigned to a group.

Race. (1) Classification of humans based on genetic characteristics; (2) Classification of people based on common nationality, history, or experiences.

Racial. (1) Of, relating to, or characteristics of race or races; 2. Arising from or based on differences among human racial groups.

Racial inferiority. The supposed lesser degree or rank of one race when compared to another.

Racial superiority. The supposed greater degree or rank of one race when compared with another.

Racially diverse. Groups comprised of people of different races.

Racism. (1) A belief that race is the primary determinant of human traits and capacities and that racial differences produce an inherent superiority of a particular race; (2) Racial prejudice or discrimination.

Religion. (1) An organized belief system based on certain tenets of faith; (2) A belief in a supreme supernatural force or god (s).

Reverse discrimination. Preferential treatment toward women and minority members in order to correct the wrongs of past racial and gender discrimination.

Sex. System of sexual classification based on biological and physical differences, such as primary and secondary sexual characteristics, forming the categories "male" and "female" as opposed to gender which is based on the social construction of the categories "men" and "women."

Sexism. Prejudice and discrimination directed at people based on gender.

Sexual harassment. Repeated unwanted sexual advances, usually toward someone subordinate to the perpetrator.

Social constructionism. A perception of an individual, group, or idea that is "constructed" through cultural and social practice, but appears to be "natural," or "the way things are." For example, the idea that women "naturally" like to do housework is a social construction because this idea appears "natural" due to its historical repetition, rather than it being "true" in any essential sense.

Socialization. To adapt people to the norms, beliefs, values, etc. of the larger group.

Stereotype. Rigid belief about groups that are held by significant numbers of people; to categorize people based on an artificial construction of a certain group designed to impart the "essence" of that group, which homogenizes the group, effacing individuality and difference.

Sub-culture. Is a group of people within a culture who practices a unique way of life, based on historical facts or generated through ideologies.

Subtle discrimination. Hidden or secret prejudicial actions or behavior.

Tolerance. Acceptance and open-mindedness to different practices, attitudes, and cultures; does not necessarily mean agreement with the differences.

Underprivileged. Applies to people who do not have the same opportunities or advantages relative to others.

Unresolved differences. Failure to bring disagreements to a successful resolution.

Visible differences. Readily apparent distinctive attributes about people.

Visible minority. A person who, based on outward appearances, is obviously a member of minority group.

White, non-Hispanic. A person having origins in any of the original peoples of Europe, North Africa, or the Middle East (except those of Hispanic origin)

White-male privilege. Advantages granted to white males above other groups.

White privilege. Advantages granted to white people above other races.

Women and minorities. The phrase commonly used to refer to women of all races and minority men.

Workforce diversity. The various racial, ethnic, and gender groups that comprise the workforce.

Appendix A
Why Diversity Training Still Matters?

By Carole Copeland Thomas
© Carole Copeland Thomas
Diversity Speaker, Trainer, and Radio Host
Carole@TellCarole.com
www.TellCarole.com
Commentary reprinted with permission of the author

Eighteen years ago when I conducted my first diversity training program, you couldn't have convinced me that more than a decade later diversity initiatives would be more valuable than ever. Remember, we were entering the golden decade of the 20th century, and the civil rights era was becoming a distant memory. Most young people of the 1990s would merely read about the achievements of the civil rights movement, in contrast to their parents who lived through those turbulent times. Affirmative Action was debated and almost tossed out with the bath water. However, case after case proved that some structure of affirmative action was needed to ensure the rights of the disadvantaged. So now that we're five years into the 21st Century is diversity still a necessary construct? YES. More than ever diversity is needed to reaffirm the principle that we should all respect and understand the differences and similarities we all share as a people.

In my book, "Personal Empowerment: How To Turbo Charge Your Life Both On And Off Your Job", I endorse the collaboration of diversity and empowerment. "Diversity and empowerment go hand in hand. Celebrating the spectrum of the human experience requires one to dig deeply into a level of personal integrity that is free of bigotry, hatred, or malice. Diversity and empowerment demand that trust and respect become an integral part of every meeting, project, relationship, negotiation or consultation that takes place between two or more people."

That's a tall order! To be free of bigotry requires purging your inner most thoughts and actions that might even remotely lead to the unfair treatment of other people. That's difficult to do, since we claim ownership to our past, our family, our values, our beliefs, and our personal perspective through our thoughts and actions.

Diversity training is needed more than ever because the world is more complex and constantly changing. Companies, resting on the laurels of their past, now find themselves caught up in mergers, acquisitions, and reorganizations. The diversity programs established a decade ago might not fit the demands of today's slimmed-down organizations. And in many cases, the diversity advocates of yesteryear are retiring, relocating, or moving on with their lives.

The world must embrace diversity, too. With over six billion people on this planet and the US a mere 5% of the world's population, we must all become more vigilant in finding new way to promote cultural understanding and enlightenment in the global marketplace. We travel to distant lands, do business across international borders, and move more freely throughout the world. That's reason enough to offer diversity training to employees, staff, association members and community builders on a regular basis.

My dream is to make my job as a diversity trainer disappear the next decade. It's a dream. And until we can figure out how to manage our differences and similarities, I'll press on promoting the virtues of diversity in this global wilderness we live in. Examine your own world and find a way to infuse diversity in everything you do. Through a lifetime of efforts, maybe my dream will come true some day.

Appendix B
A Tribute to Native American Cultural Heritage

Before Christopher Columbus landed on the shores of North America, this land was inhabited by many different Native American tribes. Although these natives were different in their ways of life, customs, and language, they shared one common belief—respect and honor for spiritual presence of the planet earth rather than mastering it.

This tradition did not last long, instead the privacy of this sacred land was intruded upon by the influx of Western Europeans who flocked the shores of this abundant land. They looked at this continent as an untouched, beautiful, yet uncultivated land with potential. However, the great problem was the existence of Native Americans who did not behave as white intruders expected. Western invaders never achieved their expectations to get rid of American Indians. They are still here with stronger ties than ever to their culture.

Historians have revealed that the Native Americans had much to say. They searched through tribal documents and found truth in the context of wisdom and rationale among those words that Native Americans left behind them. Native Americans provided us with spiritual wisdom through meaningful words that shape the way of life, for prosperity and abundance.

In North America, the Native American heritage is renowned every year in the month of November. For this special purpose, we celebrate American Indian history and the ancient culture of those who were here before us; those who valued the nature in a way that is reflected in the words of Chief Seattle Suqwamish and Duwamish: *"I was born in Nature's wide domain! The trees were all that sheltered my infant limbs, the blue heavens all that covered me. I am one of Nature's children. I have always admired her. She shall be my glory: her features, her robes, and the wreath about her brow, the seasons, her stately oaks, and the evergreen—her hair, ringlets over the earth—all contribute to my enduring love of her."*

We need to educate ourselves and encourage our children to identify the early inhabitants of this land. We should teach them that there were five nations: the Cayuga, Mohawk, Oneida, Onandaga, and Seneca which formed the Iroquois Confederation before Columbus appeared in America. These nations later became known as the Six Nations when the Tuscarora joined the Confederation. The constitution of these nations was used by Benjamin Franklin as a model for the Article of Confederation.

American Indians were three-dimensional people: physical, intellectual, and spiritual. They were religious from the first moments of life. They were lovers of nature. The Lakota was a true naturalist. The rule that *"thought comes before speech"* was the center of American Indians' philosophy of words and silence. The first Americans ardently believed in silence. Silence was the sign of total equilibrium—the absolute poise or balance of body, mind and spirit. Spiritual teaching was in order in a family institution. *"Children were taught that true politeness was to be defined in actions rather in words."* Chief Luther Standing Bear of Teton Sioux once said: " *Life was vivid and pulsing; nothing was casual and commonplace. The Indian lived—lived in every sense of the word—from his first to his last breath."*

In cultural diversity programs around the country and especially in higher education institutions in the United States, the focus is on respecting and recognizing other cultures. Today, the concept of multiculturalism replaces the old term of "the melting pot." We ought to teach our new generation the characteristics of cultural diversity starting with native Americans in early education. Diversity of cultures exists everywhere, in our schools, in our workplaces, and other public places.

William Sonnenschein [1997], the author of *The Diversity Toolkit* uses the concept of "Socialization and *ISM* Prism." For example, he suggests to place Native American in the Prism and advises that in order to better understand your socialization you need to ask yourself these questions: How were you socialized? What influenced you as you were growing up and what continues to influence you today? In this self examination typical influences include family, personal experiences, education, friends, the media, and critical incidents or events.

As we honored the "Native Americans" for their unique cultures and traditions around the country, more attention was given to the awareness and understanding of our native people who were here before us and valued this great land with their wisdom and dignity. [Today, one study reveals that, there are more than 800 communities of tribal people (Native Americans) in the country]. While Native Americans in reservations around the country are making their best efforts to gain full civil rights in this country, they are striving to recover the lost elements of their cultures and stand together to cherish their ["tribal significance]."

[1]From: Heed the Words of Wisdom, Leo Parvis, Ph.D., August 2003, Reprinted by permission of *Chaska Herald*, Minnesota.

Appendix C
Universal Declaration of Human Rights

PREAMBLE

Whereas recognition of the inherent dignity and of the equal and inalienable rights of all members of the human family is the foundation of freedom, justice and peace in the world,

Whereas disregard and contempt for human rights have resulted in barbarous acts which have outraged the conscience of mankind, and the advent of a world in which human beings shall enjoy freedom of speech and belief and freedom from fear and want has been proclaimed as the highest aspiration of the common people,

Whereas it is essential, if man is not to be compelled to have recourse, as a last resort, to rebellion against tyranny and oppression, that human rights should be protected by the rule of law,

Whereas it is essential to promote the development of friendly relations between nations,

Whereas the peoples of the United Nations have in the Charter reaffirmed their faith in fundamental human rights, in the dignity and worth of the human person and in the equal rights of men and women and have determined to promote social progress and better standards of life in larger freedom,

Whereas Member States have pledged themselves to achieve, in cooperation with the United Nations, the promotion of universal respect for and observance of human rights and fundamental freedoms,

Whereas a common understanding of these rights and freedoms is of the greatest importance for the full realization of this pledge,

Now, therefore, **The General Assembly** *proclaims*

This Universal Declaration of Human Rights

as a common standard of achievement for all peoples and all nations, to the end that every individual and every organ of society, keeping this Declaration constantly in mind, shall strive by teaching and education to promote respect for these rights and freedoms and by progressive measures, national and international, to secure their universal and effective recognition and observance, both among the peoples of Member States themselves and among the peoples of territories under their jurisdiction.

Article I

All human beings are born free and equal in dignity and rights. They are endowed with reason and conscience and should act towards one another in a spirit of brotherhood.

Article 2

Everyone is entitled to all the rights and freedoms set forth in this Declaration, without distinction of any kind, such as race, color, sex, language, religion, political or other opinion, national or social origin, property, birth or other status.

Furthermore, no distinction shall be made on the basis of the political, jurisdictional or international status of the country or territory to which a person belongs, whether it be independent, trust, non-self-governing or under any other limitation of sovereignty.

Article 3

Everyone has the right to life, liberty and security of person.

Article 4

No one shall be held in slavery or servitude; slavery and the slave trade shall be prohibited in all their forms.

Article 5

No one shall be subjected to torture or to cruel, inhuman or degrading treatment or punishment.

Article 6

Everyone has the right to recognition everywhere as a person before the law.

Article 7

All are equal before the law and are entitled without any discrimination to equal protection of the law. All are entitled to equal protection against any discrimination in violation of this Declaration and against any incitement to such discrimination.

Article 8

Everyone has the right to an effective remedy by the competent national tribunals for acts violating the fundamental rights granted him by the constitution or by law.

Article 9

No one shall be subjected to arbitrary arrest, detention or exile.

Article 10

Everyone is entitled in full equality to a fair and public hearing by an independent and impartial tribunal, in the determination of his rights and obligations and of any criminal charge against him.

Article 11

(1) Everyone charged with a penal offence has the right to be presumed innocent until proved guilty according to law in a public trial at which he has had all the guarantees necessary for his defense.

(2) No one shall be held guilty of any penal offence on account of any act or omission which did not constitute a penal offence, under national or international law, at the time when it was committed. Nor shall a heavier penalty be imposed than the one that was applicable at the time the penal offence was committed.

Article 12

No one shall be subjected to arbitrary interference with his privacy, family, home or correspondence, nor to attacks upon his honor and reputation. Everyone has the right to the protection of the law against such interference or attacks.

Article 13

(1) Everyone has the right to freedom of movement and residence within the borders of each State.

(2) Everyone has the right to leave any country, including his own, and to return to his country.

Article 14

(1) Everyone has the right to seek and to enjoy in other countries asylum from persecution.

(2) This right may not be invoked in the case of prosecutions genuinely arising from non-political crimes or from acts contrary to the purposes and principles of the United Nations.

Article 15

(1) Everyone has the right to a nationality.

(2) No one shall be arbitrarily deprived of his nationality nor denied the right to change his nationality.

Article 16

(1) Men and women of full age, without any limitation due to race, nationality or religion, have the right to marry and to found a family. They are entitled to equal rights as to marriage, during marriage and at its dissolution.

(2) Marriage shall be entered into only with the free and full consent of the intending spouses.

(3) The family is the natural and fundamental group unit of society and is entitled to protection by society and the State.

Article 17

(1) Everyone has the right to own property alone as well as in association with others.

(2) No one shall be arbitrarily deprived of his property.

Article 18

Everyone has the right to freedom of thought, conscience and religion; this right includes freedom to change his religion or belief, and freedom, either alone or in community with others and in public or private, to manifest his religion or belief in teaching, practice, worship and observance.

Article 19

Everyone has the right to freedom of opinion and expression; this right includes freedom to hold opinions without interference and to seek, receive and impart information and ideas through any media and regardless of frontiers.

Article 20

(1) Everyone has the right to freedom of peaceful assembly and association.

(2) No one may be compelled to belong to an association.

Article 21

(1) Everyone has the right to take part in the government of his country, directly or through freely chosen representatives.

(2) Everyone has the right to equal access to public service in his country.

(3) The will of the people shall be the basis of the authority of government; this shall be expressed in periodic and genuine elections which shall be by universal and equal suffrage and shall be held by secret vote or by equivalent free voting procedures.

Article 22

Everyone, as a member of society, has the right to social security and is entitled to realization, through national effort and international co-operation and in accordance with the organization and resources of each State, of the economic, social and cultural rights indispensable for his dignity and the free development of his personality.

Article 23

(1) Everyone has the right to work, to free choice of employment, to just and favorable conditions of work and to protection against unemployment.

(2) Everyone, without any discrimination, has the right to equal pay for equal work.

(3) Everyone who works has the right to just and favorable remuneration ensuring for himself and his family an existence worthy of human dignity, and supplemented, if necessary, by other means of social protection.

(4) Everyone has the right to form and to join trade unions for the protection of his interests.

Article 24

Everyone has the right to rest and leisure, including reasonable limitation of working hours and periodic holidays with pay.

Article 25

(1) Everyone has the right to a standard of living adequate for the health and well-being of himself and of his family, including food, clothing, housing and medical care and necessary social services, and the right to security in the event of unemployment, sickness, disability, widowhood, old age or other lack of livelihood in circumstances beyond his control.

(2) Motherhood and childhood are entitled to special care and assistance. All children, whether born in or out of wedlock, shall enjoy the same social protection.

Article 26

(1) Everyone has the right to education. Education shall be free, at least in the elementary and fundamental stages. Elementary education shall be compulsory. Technical and professional education shall be made generally available and higher education shall be equally accessible to all on the basis of merit.

(2) Education shall be directed to the full development of the human personality and to the strengthening of respect for human rights and fundamental freedoms. It shall promote understanding, tolerance and friendship among all nations, racial or religious groups, and shall further the activities of the United Nations for the maintenance of peace.

(3) Parents have a prior right to choose the kind of education that shall be given to their children.

Article 27

(1) Everyone has the right freely to participate in the cultural life of the community, to enjoy the arts and to share in scientific advancement and its benefits.

(2) Everyone has the right to the protection of the moral and material interests resulting from any scientific, literary or artistic production of which he is the author.

Article 28

Everyone is entitled to a social and international order in which the rights and freedoms set forth in this Declaration can be fully realized.

Article 29

(1) Everyone has duties to the community in which alone the free and full development of his personality is possible.

(2) In the exercise of his rights and freedoms, everyone shall be subject only to such limitations as are determined by law solely for the purpose of securing due recognition and respect for the rights and freedoms of others and of meeting the just requirements of morality, public order and the general welfare in a democratic society.

(3) These rights and freedoms may in no case be exercised contrary to the purposes and principles of the United Nations.

Article 30

Nothing in this Declaration may be interpreted as implying for any State, group or person any right to engage in any activity or to perform any act aimed at the destruction of any of the rights and freedoms set forth herein.

G.A. res. 217A (III), U.N. Doc A/810 at 71 (1948)

Adopted on December 10, 1948
by the General Assembly of the United Nations (without dissent)

Appendix D

Resources

Web Sites: General Subjects

www.udhr.org - Human Rights Campaign

www.umd.edu - University of Maryland Web Site

www.diversityinc.com - Very Resourceful On-line Diversity Magazine

www.diversityweb.org - An Interactive Resource Hub for Higher Education

www.crede.org – Center for Research on Education, Diversity, and Excellence

www.about.com – Passionate People with Practical Advice and Solutions

www.religioustolerance.org -Ontario Consultants promoting religious understanding, tolerance and freedom

On Hate Crime and Discrimination
www.apa.org - American Psychological Association.
www.adl.org - Anti-Defamation League
www.splcenter.org - Southern Poverty Law Center Publication
www.pbs.org - PBS: Not In Our Town.
www.usdoj.gov - FBI Background on Hate Crimes
www.ngltf.org - Nat'l Gay & Lesbian Task Force
www.matthewshepard.org - Matthew Shepard Foundation.
www.pflag.org - Parents, Family, and Friends of Lesbians and Gays
www.gladd.org - The Gay and Lesbian Alliance against Defamation
www.wiesenthal.com -The Simon Wiesenthal Center
www.ed.gov - U.S. Dept. of Education: Preventing Youth Hate Crimes

- 194 -

www.avp.org - The NYC Gay & Lesbian Anti-Violence Project
www.hatecrime.org - National Center for Hate Crime Prevention
www.cphv.usm.maine.edu -Center for the Prevention of Hate Violence
www.truthcenter.net - The National Hate Crime Alert Center
www.itvs.org - On-line PBS: Forgotten Fires
www.hate.com - HBO: Hate.com
www.adc.org -The American-Arab Anti-Discrimination Committee

Videos:

America Needs Human Rights: Food First
A Time for Justice: Teachingtolernace.org
Communicating Between Cultures: Learning Seed
Dakota Conflict: KTCA, St. Paul, MN
Daughters of Afghanistan: Video Service Corporation (VSC) and
(dis)Ability Awareness: Learning Seed
Ellis Island, I, II, and III: A &E
Everybody's Ethnic: Learning Seed
Food: A Multi-Cultural Feast: Learning Seed
Forgotten Fires: PBS
Global Eating: Learning Seed
How the World Dresses: Learning Seed
Mighty Times; Story of Rosa Parks: Teachingtolernace.org
MLK Commemorative Collection: MPI Home Video
Muslims: The Independent Production Fund Inc.
Not in My Town: Universal
The Children's March: Teachingtolernace.org
Them And Us: Learning seed
The Shadow of Hate: Teaching Tolerance
Understanding Our Differences: Learning Seed

References

Abu-Jaber, D. (2003). *Crescent: A Romance in Iran-geles,* New York, NY: W. W. Norton Publishing Inc.

Abu-Laban, Y. and Gabriel, C. (2002). *Selling Diversity*, Peterborough, Ontario, Canada: Broadview Press.

Adams, M., Bell, L.A., & Griffin, P. (Eds.). (1997). *Teaching for Diversity and Social Justice*, New York & London: Routledge.

Alba, R. D. (1992). Ethnicity. In E. F. Borgotta & M. L. Borgotta, (Eds.), *Encyclopedia of Sociology, 1*, 575-584. New York: McMillan.

Alessandra, T. and Hunsaker, P. (1993). *Communication at Work*, New York, NY: Simon and Schuster (A Fireside Book).

Arrien, A. (Ed.). (2001). *Working Together: Diversity as Opportunity,* San Francisco, CA: Berrett-Koehler Publishers.

Asante, M. K. (2002). *100 Greatest African Americans: A Biographical Encyclopedia.* Amherst, NY: Prometheus Books.

Benhabib, S. (2002). *The Claims of Culture*. Princeton, NJ: Princeton University Press.

Bhagwati, J. (2004). *In Defense of Globalization*, New York, NY: Oxford University Press.

Boyd, A. (Ed.). (1997). *Guide to Multicultural Resources*, Fort Atkinson, WI: Highsmith Press.

Calvin. J. (2001). Leadership diversity. In A. Arrien, (Ed.), *Working Together: Diversity as Opportunity,* San Francisco, CA: Berrett-Koehler Publishers.

Cascio, W. (2003). *Managing Human Resources.* (6th ed.), New York, NY: McGraw-Hill.

Casey, K. and Vanceburg, M. *The Promise of a New Day*, New York, NY: Harper/Hazelden.

Chafe, W. (Ed.) (2003). *A History of Our Time*, (6th ed.), New York, NY: Oxford University Press, Inc.

Chinadaily.com (2005). Mc Donald's revamps menu, expands in China, in www.chinadaily.com

Ching, C. (2003). *Personal Voices: Facing Up to Race*, AlterNet.

CIA (2005). The Types of Government, *The World Factbook,* www.cia.gov / publications/ factbook.

Coppenger, M. (2002). *First-Person: Baha'ism: nudging toward becoming America's religion*, www.sbcbaptistpress.org

De Botton, A. (1999). *The Essential Plato*. Jowett, B. (trans.). New York, NY: Quality Paperback Book Club.

De Vito. J (1982). *Communicology: An Introduction to the Study of Communication*, New York, NY: Harper and Row

Diller, J. (1999). *Cultural Diversity: A Primer for the Human Services*, Belmont, CA: Wadsworth Publishing Company.

DiversityInc.Com (2005). Father of Affirmative Action Arthur Fletcher Dies, Washington DC: DiversityInc.com. July 14.

DiversityInc.Com (2005). , Color Commentary: Oprah's Wealth Doesn't Protect Her From Racism. Washington DC: DiversityInc.com, July 12.

DOJ (Department of Justice). (1996). *Training Guide for Hate Crime Data Collection: Uniform Crime Reporting*, FBI, Criminal Justice Information Service Division, Washington DC, U.S. Department of Justice.

Encyclopedia Britannica (2005). Natural Law, Encyclopedia Britannica Premium Service.

Etzioni, A. (1996). *The New Golden Rule: Community and Morality in a Democratic Society*, New York: Basic Books.

Flowers, N., Bernbaum, M., Rudelius-Palmer, K. and Tolman, J. (2000) *The Human Rights Education Handbook*, Minneapolis, MN: University of Minnesota, Human Rights Resource Center and the Stanley Foundation.

Ford, C.W. (1994). *We can all get along: 50 Steps You Can Take to Help End Racism.* Dell Publishing Company.

Forni, P.M. (2002). *Choosing Civility: The Twenty Five Rules of Considerate Conduct,* New York, NY: St. Martin's Press.

Garcia, E. (2002). *Student Cultural Diversity: Understanding and Meeting the Challenge.* (3rd. ed.), New York: Houghton Mifflin Company.

Gentile, M. C. (Ed.) (2000). *Differences That Work: Organizational Excellence through Diversity*, Prospect Heights, IL: Waveland Press, Inc.

Grabhorn, L. (2000). *Excuse Me, Your Life is Waiting,* Charlottesville, VA: Hampton Roads Publishing Co.

Griggs, L. B. and Louw, L. L. (1995). (Eds.). *Valuing Diversity: New Tools for a New Reality*, New York, NY: McGraw Hills.

Guralnik, D. B. (Ed.) (1986). *Webster's New World Dictionary of the American Language,* New York, NY: Simon and Schuster.

Haessly, J. (2001). A Journey toward inclusion. In A. Arrien, (Ed.), *Working Together: Diversity as Opportunity,* San Francisco, CA: Berrett-Koehler Publishers.

Hartin,E. (1997). *Plessy v.Ferguson,* 1892, www.northpark.edu

Heuberger, B. (2001). *Cultural Diversity: Building Skills for Awareness, Understanding and Application.* (2nd ed.), Dubuque, IA: Kendall/Hunt Publishing Company.

Hill Harper, M. & Appel, W. S. (2001). Living and Loving in a Diverse World. In A. Arrien, (Ed.). (2001). *Working Together: Diversity as Opportunity,* San Francisco, CA: Berrett-Koehler Publishers.

Hogan-Garcia, M. (2003). *The Four Skills of Cultural Diversity Competence.* (2nd ed.), Pacific Grove, CA: Brooks/Cole-Thompson Learning.

Hsiao, H. (2002). "Coexistence and Synthesis: Cultural Globalization and Localization in Contemporary Taiwan" in Berger P. and Huntington, S. (Eds.), *Many Globalizations: Cultural Diversity in the Contemporary World*, New York, NY: Oxford University Press.

Human Rights Watch (2003). http://www.hrw.org/reports/2002/us911/

Ippoliti, E. (2004). *At the Heart of Human Rights Education: The Universal Declaration of Human Rights*, www.chrf.ca Jost, D. A., et al. (1993) *American Heritage College Dictionary*, (3rded.),NewYork, NY: Houghton Mifflin Company.

King, M. L. (1968). I Have a Dream, *The Peaceful Warrior*, New York, NY: Pocket Books

Kornblum, J. & Julian, J. (2004). *Social Problems.* (11th ed.). Upper Saddle River, NJ:Pearson Prentice Hall.

Kurtz, H. (2005). "Newsweek Records Guantanamo Bay Story", May 17, 2005, P. A03, *Washington Post.*

Lafair, S. (2001). The Inside Out Project: Diversity and the Human Psyche. In A. Arrien, (Ed.).*Working Together: Diversity as Opportunity,* San Francisco, CA: Berrett-Koehler Publishers.

Larmer, R. A. (1996). *Ethics in the Workplace: Selected Readings in Business Ethics.* St. Paul, MN: West Publishing Company

Laroche, L. (2003). *Managing Cultural Diversity in Technical Professions*, Butterworth-Burlington, MA: Heinemann, an Imprint of Elsevier Science.

Legal Information Institute. (2003).School of Law, Cornell University, Ithaca, NY.

Lindsey, L. & Beach, S. (2002). *Sociology.* (2nd ed.). Upper Saddle River, NJ: Prentice-Hall.

Live8technorati.com (2005), What is Live 8?, www.live8tecnorati.com

Luhabe, N. W. (2001). Bridging the Gap. In A. Arrien, (Ed.). *Working Together: Diversity as Opportunity,* San Francisco, CA: Berrett-Koehler Publishers.

Massaro, D. R. (1996). Italian American as a cognizable racial group. In J. Kromkowski (Ed.), *Race and Ethnic Relations* (6th ed., pp. 187-191). Guilford, CT: Dushkin Publishing Group.

Mastrianna, F. V. & Hailstones, T. J. (1998). *Basic Economics.* (11th ed.), Cincinnati, OH: South-Western College Publishing.

Matlin, M. W. (1999). (3rd. ed.). *Psychology*, Orlando, FL.: Harcourt Brace & Company.

Mazel. E. (1998). *And don't call me a racist.* Lexington, MA: Argonaut Press.

Malkin, M. (2005). "Guantanamo Bay: The Rest of the Story", May 26, 2005 issue, *www.michellemalkin.com*

Meyerson, D. E. and Fletcher, J. K. (2001). A modest Manifesto for Shattering the Glass Ceiling, In *Harvard Business Review on Managing Diversity*, Boston, MA: Harvard Business School Press.

Middleton, D. (2003). *The Challenge of Human Diversity: Mirrors, Bridges, and Chasms.* (2nd ed.), Prospect Heights, IL: Waveland Press Inc.

Mittal, A. and Rosset, P. (Eds.) (1999). *America Needs Human Rights*, Oakland, CA: Food First Books.

Mnadvocates.org (2004). Dispelling the Myths about Immigrants, Minneapolis, MN: Minnesota Advocates for Human Rights, www.mnadvocates.org

Murdoch, G. (1945). The common denominator of culture. In Ralph Linton (Ed.), *The Science of Man in World Crisis*. New York, NY: Columbia University.

National Geographic. (2002). *Family Reference Atlas of the World,* Washington, D.C.: National Geographic Society.

Nerburn, K. & Mengelkoch, L. (Eds.). (1991). *Native American Wisdom*, San Rafael, CA: New World Library.

NOW (2004). The *Constitutional Equality Amendment (*CEA), National Organization for Women, www.now.org.

Parvis, L. (2003). Diversity and Effective Leadership in Multicultural Workplaces, *Journal of Environmental Health*, 65(7).

..............(2003). How Much of the "Dream" Has Become a Reality?: A Tribute to Martin Luther King, *Chaska Herald,* Chaska, MN.

…………..(2005). Putting Synergy to Work, *Minnesota Business*, 15(3), 62.

Pattillo Beals, M. (2002). *Warriors Don't Cry*, New York, NY: Simon Pulse.

Randeria, P. E. (2001). In A. Arrien, (Ed.), *Working Together: Diversity as Opportunity,* San Francisco, CA: Berrett-Koehler Publishers.

Rich, T. (2004). *Judaism 101*, www.jewfaq.org.

Schrag, P. (1996). So You Want To Be Color-Blind: Alternative Principles for   Affirmative Action. In J. Kromkowski (Ed.), *Race and Ethnic Relations* (6th ed., pp.158-163). Guilford, CT: Dushkin Publishing Group.

Scupin, R. (2003). *Cultural Anthropology: A Global Perspective.* Upper Saddle Rive, NJ: Prentice-Hall. (5th ed.). Upper Saddle River, NJ: Prentice-Hall.

Shepard, J. (1996). *Sociology.* (6th ed.). St. Paul, MN: West Publishing Company.

Shepard, J. (2003). *Sociology.* (8th ed.). St. Paul, MN: West Publishing Company.

Simons, G. (2002). *Working Together: Succeeding in a Multicultural Organization*, (3rd ed.), Menlo Park, CA: Crisp Learning.

Sonnenschein, W. (1997). *The Diversity Toolkit,* Chicago, IL: Contemporary Books.

Srinivas, T. (2002). "A Tryst with Destiny" in Berger P. and Huntington, S. (Eds.), *Many Globalizations: Cultural Diversity in the Contemporary World*, New York, NY: Oxford University Press.

Star Tribune (2001). *Migration to Minnesota from Around the World.* Star Tribune Map, October 22, 2002.

Takaki, R. (1993). *A Different Mirror: A History of Multicultural America*, Boston, MA: Little Brown and Company.

Thomas, D. A. & Alderfer, C.P. (1988), The Significance of Race and Ethnicity for Understanding Organizational Behavior. In C. Cooper (Ed.) *Review of Industrial and Organizational Psychology,* New York, NY: John Wiley & Sons.

Thomas, R. R. Jr. (1996). *Redefining Diversity.* New York, NY: AMACOM, a division of   American Management Association.

USA Today (2005). America the Diverse: Annual Travel report, May 13-15, 2005, usaweekend.com

Walsh, B. (2005). International Themes: Quotes on Globalization, *www.tcnj.edu*

Watts, V. (2004). Personal interview with Veronica Watts, Director of Diversity, General Mills, MN.

Welch Shrank, L. (1995). *Valuing diversity: multicultural communication*, Lake Zurich, IL: The Learning Seed.

Williams, J. (2002). *Eyes on the Prize*, New York, NY: Penguin Books.

Williams, S. (2001). Recipes for Synergy, In A. Arrien, (Ed.), *Working Together: Diversity as Opportunity,* San Francisco, CA: Berrett-Koehler Publishers.

www.tcnj.edu (2004). Quotes on Globalization, www. tcnj.edu.

www.racerelations.about.com (2005). Hate Crime Legislation, www.about.com

www.usm.edu (2000). Timeline, Center for Oral History and Cultural Heritage at the University of Southern Mississippi. www-dept.usm.edu/

Yan, Y. (2002). "Managed Globalization" in Berger P. and Huntington, S. (Eds.), *Many Globalizations: Cultural Diversity in the Contemporary World*, New York, NY: Oxford University Press.

diversitypromotions.com

Help us spread the word:

"Embrace Diversity, Embrace Our World"

For products featuring the stunning full-color "Embrace Diversity" logo and other products promoting positive messages about diversity, please visit our website at www.diversitypromotions.com. Our products can be used in all of your special events celebrating cultural diversity, human rights, and multiculturalism.

We have been successful in establishing "National Diversity Day" which is the first Friday in October (Diversity Awareness Month). We encourage you to have your own National Diversity Day celebration at your school, place of worship, work or home—we are all diverse in our many wonderful ways—let's celebrate those things that make us the same and different! We are all one in one nation, the most beautifully diverse nation in the world! For ideas on how to celebrate National Diversity Day, please go to our website: www.nationaldiversityday.com

For more information, contact us at: drparvis@diversitypromotions.com or marketingdiva@diversitypromotions.com

Index

A
Ableism, 68
Abu-Jaber, 6
Accommodation, 113
Acculturation, 34
Affirmative-action, 17, 72-73, 79, 179
African American, 39
Ageism, 60-61, 66-67, 80
AHANA (African, Hispanic/Latino, Asian/Pacific Islander, and Native American), 60
American Civil Liberties Union (ACLU), 60
Americans with Disabilities Act (ADA), 68
Anti-Defamation League, 48, 51, 60
Asia Pacific Center, 60
Asian, 63, 73,105, 112, 115, 150, 155
Asian American, 6, 42
Assimilation, 32-33
Avoidance, 113

B
Babariga, 72
Baby Boomers, 67
Baha'i, 109
Beals, Melba Pattillo, 69, 87, 96
Bias, 48
Bigotry, 46-47, 49-50, 53-54, 89, 97, 144, 179
Birmingham Pledge, 55
Bloody Sunday, 93
Bond, Julian, 83-84
Brokaw, Tom, 68
Brown vs. Board of Education, 85
Buddhism, 108

C
Christianity, 107
Civil Rights Legislation, 83

Civility, 124
Class, 17, 20, 22, 48, 61, 63, 65, 78,127
Classism, 60-62, 65, 79, 127
Collaboration, 114
Conflict, 16, 94, 112-114
Critical thinking, 47
Cultural universals, 2
Culture shock, 7
Culture, summary of, 10

D

Dashiki, 72
Declaration of Tolerance, 54
Denigration, 48, 53, 64
Diaspora, 108
Disabled and handicapped, 68
Diversity, definition of, 15
Domination, 113

E

Employment discrimination, 70
Enculturation, 31, 38
Equal Employment Opportunity (EEO), 70
Equal Employment Opportunity Commission (EEOC), 70
Erickson, Lee B., 82, 102, 134
Ethnicity, 4-10, 18-23, 31, 40, 48, 52-53, 60, 74, 108
Ethnocentrism, 5, 22, 132
Etiquette, 3
Etzioni, Amitai, 7
Eurocentrism, 31
Exclusion, 33, 61, 128

F

Feminism, 66
Freedom Riders, 87
Freedom Summer, 93

G

Gender, 18

T
Tolerance, 17

U
Universal Declaration of Human Rights (UDHR), 137, 151-152
University of Mississippi, 87
Urban League, 60

V
Values, 3-5, 10, 18, 32, 35, 50, 65, 67, 74, 105, 110, 124, 149, 156-157, 159-160, 179
Vespucci, Amerigo, 8

W
White Privilege, 65
Woolworth's Incident, 87
World Trade Organization (WTO), 158, 16

Y
Yarmulke, 72
Yoga, 74, 158
Yogananda, Paramahansa, 7

Z
Zoroastrian, 107, 113, 123